"they

look at you and are revulsed.

"They call you ***freaks*** and they think your handicaps are all there is to who you ***are***!

"We can prove them *wrong*. We can turn their scorn to grudging admiration.

"***Join*** with me, my friends. ***Together*** we can make a ***difference***."

— from "The Secret Origin of the Doom Patrol."

doom PATROL

writer grant morrison

pencillers richard case
doug braithwaite

inkers scott hanna
carlos garzon
john nyberg

colorists daniel vozzo
michele wolfman

letterer john workman

original series covers
richard case
scott hanna
carlos garzon

nobody

DOOM PATROL: **CRAWLING FROM THE WRECKAGE**

Published by DC Comics. DC Comics, 1700 Broadway, New York, NY 10019. A Warner Bros. Entertainment Company. Printed in Canada. Second Printing. ISBN: 1-56389-034-8 Cover illustration by **Brian Bolland**. Publication design by **John J. Hill**.

wants to be a human brain in a **robot** body

or

why this isn't a super-hero comic, and **why** that's good

But enough about DOOM PATROL; let's talk about me.

When I was a kid, like millions of others, I would pin a red bath towel to my collar and imitate Georg Reeves's springboard Superman takeoffs. Other days, unlike millions of others, I might clench my right fist and spin my arm like a windmill, creating a miniature tornado that could uproot trees, in imitation of the Flash's super-speed. Sometimes, like no other kid before or since, I would wear my sport coat and clip-on necktie and dart for cover from bush to car to tree as I believed James Bond would if he ever ended up in my neighborhood. Besides absorbing and reliving the adventures of these beloved heroes, I also read Arnold Drake and Bruno Premiani's DOOM PATROL each month — but I never wrapped my head in bandages and feigned weakness in 60-second bursts as a radioactive parasite fled my body to perform routine rescues that I could only watch. I never wished that isolated parts of my body could grow or shrink if only I could concentrate hard enough. I certainly never wanted to burn to a crisp in an auto wreck so my brain could be transplanted into a clunky robot body with a steamshovel jaw.

And that's why the Doom Patrol — Larry Trainor, Negative Man; Rita Farr, Elasti-Girl; and Cliff Steele, Robotman — weren't really super-heroes, despite their names and the way they looked. Part of the function of a super-hero is to give us a refuge from our normalcy, an identification with something wonderful, a secret airborne headquarters from which we can look down at our friends, families and authority figures — especially authority figures — and feel pity for their tragic lack of special gifts.

Disguised as a regular comic book, DOOM PATROL subverted this drive. Compared to the omniplegic Cliff and the infected Larry, normal people were to be envied, not pitied. In a similar way, a nine-year-old who windmills his arm in the direction of an old elm tree on a busy city street corner in broad daylight might secretly envy normal people as they puzzle at him from their Valiants and Corvairs. Maybe you have felt this envy, too.

So if the Doom Patrol aren't super-heroes, I guess they're people, just like you and me, or at least like me. They don't look like anything that can exist, but maybe the feelings that come with the full-body bandages and the steamshovel jaw and the ankles like sequoia trunks are as genuine as the last time you compared yourself to a stranger and came up short. Maybe the untroubled normalcy we project onto others is what's so preposterous. Maybe the Doom Patrol make perfect sense.

Mind you, I'm not claiming to have developed this analysis 29 years ago while amputating the pet parakeet's wings for my homemade Hawkman helmet*; all I really knew then was that the DP were gross and made me feel weird, and that I went out of my way to buy every issue.

It's almost thirty years later, and Grant Morrison and Richard Case have given us a new Doom Patrol (whose story begins in this volume), and interested readers have an opportunity to feel gross and weird all over again. Like the original version, Grant and Richard's Doom Patrol sort of resemble other action heroes on the surface, but fall pathetically out of step once the chase music starts. Crime-fighters who fly,

*Just kidding, bird-lovers

shrink and stretch once again seem ordinary by comparison, and ordinary people lucky. Their first full storyline, "Crawling From the Wreckage," begins in one hospital and cuts abruptly to another, racking up infirmities in the first few pages like most comic books go through super-powers.

In the place of Rita, who could pass for regular folks, and whose power was never all that horrible, there's Kay Challis, the unforgettable Crazy Jane, whose paranormal "gifts" are limited only by the number of personalities serving time inside her head. As her story opens, there are 64 in attendance.

Larry Trainor and the super-parasite are still together, joined by the unwilling Dr. Eleanor Poole to form Rebis, the radioactive hermaphrodite who just doesn't sound like Larry anymore. That bothers our old friend Cliff; he's still the same, but when you start out as a leaky gray sponge in a prosthetic body there's not much room to deteriorate.

Also along for the plunge are Niles Caulder, the difficult genius who founded the Doom Patrol; Rhea Jones, a comatose girl who seems to be sleeping her way toward a frightening destiny; and the lovable Dorothy Spinner, an ape-faced adolescent whose inner life can manifest itself for all to see — a "gift" that would have most teenagers clawing the asylum gate for entry.

The only member with what I would call healthy, average super-powers — Joshua Clay, a physician who can fly and shoot some kind of ray-blasts from his fists — is too freaked-out by all of this to let himself use them. He'd rather stand by for the inevitable medical emergencies and perform routine tasks for the Chief in the meantime.

As tedious as that sounds, we can't blame Josh for trading his tights for an apron when we consider the opposition. The Doom Patrol has never been lucky enough to face mere jewel thieves who dress like playing cards, or masked kidnappers who messenger easy clues to their whereabouts to the commissioner's office. Their rogues gallery is more likely to include the imaginary world that threatens to become real, supplanting our own reality; the unattended machine that could make dreams come true; the bloodthirsty omnipotent who claims to be God, and who's to say for sure he's lying?

For all of these dangerous encounters, for all of our heroes' disorders and infirmities, for all of their fear and heartbreak, one of the best features of Grant's DOOM PATROL scripts is what's missing from them. Another writer working with the same ingredients might have inflated the stories with the familiar grim-and-gritty solemnity of the DARK KNIGHT/WATCHMEN imitators. Don't bother looking for the (yawn) clipped, first-person angst, the (groan) balletic violence, the (sob) dead

sidekicks, the (ah-chooo!) anguished resignation that worked so well in those projects and has seldom done the job since. Grant is too playful and hard-working a writer for any of this; in its place, you'll find pleasure in the strange workings of his universe, a fondness for its inhabitants, and a straightforward presentation rare in comics today.

A large share of the credit for that presentation must go to Richard Case's style and storytelling. Watching him grow from the raw but confident talent seen here to the inspired practitioner of the current run has been one of DOOM PATROL's most satisfying rewards.

The result of Richard and Grant's hard work is one of my favorite comics ever. A couple of years after these stories were first published, I had the good fortune to become editor of the regular monthly title. No matter what happens, I intend to hang on to DOOM PATROL until they pry it from my cold, dead fingers.

But enough about me; let's read DOOM PATROL.

—Tom Peyer

1992

"All the time I've been away, I've been studying reports, filing information, making

preparations"

NEW FORMAT
19
FEB 89
$1.50
$1.85
UK 80p
THE
DOOM
PATROL
CRAWLING
FROM THE
WRECKAGE
PART 1 OF 4
by GRANT MORRISON
RICHARD CASE
& CARLOS GARZON
CHASE & GARZON

roaringraringracing haring home on the homestretch now and the wind in my ears the sound of the crowd
DEAN TIRES
COLLEEN'S COOKIES
200 on the speedo...210... 215...220...and oh the sky runningspilling blue smoke
NIKON
every-thing moves
36
so
slow
and i should have seen it
the oil slick
i should have
saved it
i saved it
i saved the beautiful bit
PORSCHE

CRAWLING FROM THE WRECKAGE

AAUUUUUUUUGH!

WELL, NOW...

DREAMING ABOUT OUR ACCIDENT AGAIN, ARE WE?
THAT'S WHAT HAPPENS...
...WHEN WE REFUSE TO TAKE OUR MEDICATION.
GET LOST.

COME ON NOW, RISE AND SHINE! I'VE BROUGHT YOU A FRESH NUTRIENT TANK.
NOW WHERE ARE WE GOING TO PUT IT?

"WE" CAN SHOVE IT WHERE THE SUN DOESN'T SHINE.
HARD.

YOU'VE GOT A REAL BAD ATTITUDE PROBLEM, MISTER. I'LL TELL YOU THAT FOR NOTHING.
SHUT UP.
GET OUT.

JUST LEAVE ME ALONE.

ALAMANCE
MEMORIAL
HOSPITAL

...YES, THIS IS **ELEANOR POOLE**...WELL, IF YOU LIKE... **THE** ELEANOR POOLE.
...OF COURSE... WELL, **YOUR** REPUTATION PRECEDES YOU ...I'M AFRAID SO, YEAH...
TRANSPLANT
9C

WHAT?... YOU READ **THAT?** OH, WELL...NOW YOU'RE EMBARRASSING **ME.**
ANYWAY, WHAT CAN I DO FOR YOU?
LARRY TRAINOR, RIGHT.
WELL, YOU'LL BE GLAD TO KNOW THAT HE'S IN GREAT SHAPE AND WE HOPE TO SEND HIM HOME IN THE NEXT DAY OR TWO...THAT'S RIGHT...
YEAH...UH, LISTEN. SOMETHING'S JUST... YEAH.
GREAT TALKING TO YOU, TOO... SURE. FINE.
YOU, TOO.
BYE.

WELL.
TWO CALLS COVERED EVERYTHING, I THINK. LARRY'S FINE, RHEA STILL HASN'T COME OUT OF HER COMA, AND I HAVE AN APPOINTMENT WITH MY PHYSIO-THERAPIST ON FRIDAY.
HAVE YOU CONSIDERED MY OFFER YET, JOSHUA?
I DON'T THINK SO, CAULDER. THAT'S NOT WHY I'M HERE.
2
I REALLY JUST DROPPED BY TO SEE HOW EVERY-ONE WAS, YOU KNOW?
AND TO SAY GOODBYE TO THE OLD PLACE.
2
A&M MOVING
OFFICIAL DOOM PATROL STUFF

SO YOU WON'T JOIN MY NEW DOOM PATROL, IS THAT WHAT YOU'RE SAYING?
DOOM PATROL

LOOK, THE DOOM PATROL'S DEAD, CAULDER. WHY NOT LET IT REST IN PEACE THIS TIME?

AND AS FOR ME, I'M FINISHED WITH ALL THIS. REALLY.
IT'S JUST NOT FUNNY ANYMORE.

ARANI'S DEAD, SCOTT'S DEAD, RHEA'S IN A COMA, LARRY'S HOSPITALIZED, VAL'S RESIGNED, AND NO ONE'S EVEN MENTIONED CLIFF...
CLIFF SIGNED HIMSELF INTO A PSYCHIATRIC HOSPITAL. HE FELT HE NEEDED HELP.

I SHOULDN'T WORRY. I'VE ASKED A GOOD FRIEND TO PAY HIM A VISIT.
AND I'M SURE IT WON'T BE LONG BEFORE ROBOTMAN IS BACK WITH US AGAIN.
JEEZ, BUT YOU'RE AN ICEMAN, CAULDER.
WHY THANK YOU, JOSHUA. AND PLEASE...
...CALL ME CHIEF.

CHICKEN THAT LAYS AN EGG WITH THE FACE OF *CHRIST* IMPRINTED ON THE SHELL, INHUMAN VOICES WHISPERING THROUGH THE STATIC ON AN EMPTY RADIO WAVEBAND.
DON'T THESE THINGS *FASCINATE* YOU, JOSHUA?

NOT REALLY. I CAN GET *THAT* KIND OF STUFF FROM THE *NATIONAL ENQUIRER.*
B-3
AND I DON'T SEE WHAT IT HAS TO DO WITH THE DOOM PATROL.

I HAVE PLANS, JOSHUA. ALL THE TIME I'VE BEEN AWAY, I'VE BEEN STUDYING REPORTS, FILING INFORMATION, MAKING *PREPARATIONS.*
B-3
KLIK

AND DON'T TELL ME—WHETHER I LIKE IT OR NOT, I'M PART OF THE BIG PLAN, RIGHT?
B-3

OH, YES.
YOU *ALL* ARE.

MR. STEELE?

MR. STEELE, YOU HAVE A VISITOR HERE TO SEE YOU.
CLIFF?

CLIFF, IT'S ME.

IT'S WILL. WILL MAGNUS.
YOU REMEMBER ME, DON'T YOU?

I MADE THE METAL MEN, CLIFF.
I MADE YOUR BODY, TOO, REMEMBER?

CLIFF?
UH... RIGHT.
YEAH.

I KNEW I RECOGNIZED THAT PATRONIZING TONE FROM SOME-WHERE.

THERE'S NO NEED FOR THAT, CLIFF.
WHEN I HEARD YOU'D COME IN HERE, I... WELL, I UNDERSTAND WHAT YOU'RE GOING THROUGH. I'VE BEEN THERE.

AND I THINK YOU AND I CAN LICK THIS THING TOGETHER.
HOW ABOUT IT, CLIFF?

YOU'RE A GOOD GUY, DOC.
YOU'RE SENSITIVE AND CARING AND COMPASSIONATE.

AND IF I COULD, I'D SPEW IN YOUR FACE.

TOMORROW? AND I WAS JUST GETTING USED TO ALL THE **ATTENTION.**

WE NOTICED.

SO GIVE IT TO ME STRAIGHT, DOC.

HOW LONG HAVE I GOT?

SAME AS EVERYONE ELSE, LARRY. NO MORE, NO LESS.

YOU STILL HAVE WHAT EVERYONE'S CALLING THE "HERO GENE," BUT APART FROM THAT, YOU'RE PERFECTLY NORMAL.

YOU BET I AM!

WHEN ALL THIS IS OVER, YOU AND ME OUGHT TO GET TOGETHER, DOCTOR, YOU KNOW THAT?

LISTEN, IT COULD BE OVER SOONER THAN YOU THINK...

...IF MY BOYFRIEND HEARS YOU TALKING LIKE THAT.

AND REMEMBER, THAT BELL BESIDE THE BED'S ONLY FOR **EMERGENCIES,** OKAY?

YEAH. SURE THING, DOCTOR.

SEE YOU.

PARTNERS IN WONDER

LAARREEE

LAARRREEEE

OH, GOD.

WHAT DO YOU WANT?
...WHAT...
OH, GOD.

IAMTHE SPIRITINTHE BOTTLETHE INVISIBLEFIRE THATWORKSIN SECRETTHERE ISTICKAMONG THEROOTSOF THEOAKTREE
OPENTHE WINDOWNOW
OPENTHE WINDOWLAR RYLETMEIN
LETMEIN
LET
ME
IN

...WHY D'YOU KEEP FOLLOWING ME ABOUT, MAGNUS?
YOU'VE GOT TO PULL YOURSELF THROUGH THIS, CLIFF!
WHY DON'T YOU JUST LEAVE ME ALONE?
BELIEVE ME, I KNOW WHAT IT'S LIKE...

HOW THE HELL CAN YOU "YOU KNOW WHAT IT'S LIKE"!?
HOW CAN YOU KNOW WHAT IT'S LIKE TO HAVE YOUR BRAIN TRANS-PLANTED INTO A METAL BODY? IT'S LIFE IMPRISONMENT!
CAN YOU IMAGINE HOW CRUDE ROBOT SENSES ARE, COMPARED TO HUMAN ONES, HUH? ALL I HAVE ARE MEMORIES OF THE WAY THINGS USED TO FEEL OR TASTE.
YOU KNOW, THEY SAY THAT AMPUTEES FEEL PHANTOM PAINS WHERE THEIR LIMBS USED TO BE. WELL, I'M A TOTAL AMPU-TEE.
I'M HAUNTED BY THE GHOST OF MY ENTIRE BODY! I GET HEADACHES, YOU KNOW, AND I WANT TO CRAP UN-TIL I REALIZE I DON'T HAVE ANY BOWELS.
AND...WHEN I LOOK AT A WOMAN, SOME-TIMES I...
BUT SURELY THE DOOM PATROL HELPED TO...

THE DOOM PATROL? DON'T TALK TO ME...IT... THE DOOM PATROL KILLS PEOPLE. IT CHEWS THEM UP AND VOMITS OUT THE BITS.
IT KILLED RITA AND ARANI AND SCOTT...

CLIFF...
I JUST CAN'T STAND ANYMORE... I CAN'T GET THROUGH IT... REALLY...
I CAN'T.

LISTEN, CLIFF, YOU'VE GOT TO PULL YOURSELF TOGETHER. THERE ARE DRUGS... ANTI-DEPRESSANTS...
I CAN'T STAND BY AND WATCH YOU DESTROY YOURSELF!

COLLEEN
DIE
CLIFF!
ME? HOW CAN I DESTROY MYSELF?
WATCH!

SEE!
CLIFF, FOR GOD'S SAKE!
NOTHING! I CAN'T FEEL ANYTHING!!

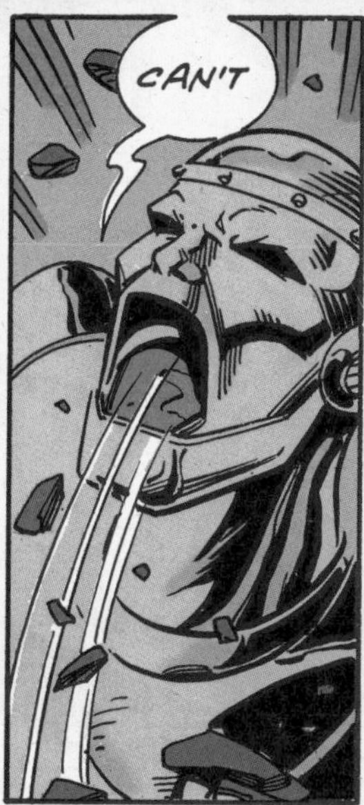
CAN'T

FEEL
ANY-THING!

CAN'T FEEL ANY-THING
OH, GOD.

OH, GOD. MAKE IT STOP.
PLEASE.

FOX
STOP.

...BUT YOU'VE NEVER SPOKEN BEFORE. I DON'T UNDERSTAND...
ALAMANCE MEMORIAL HOSPITAL

PER HAPSIHAD NOTHINGTO SAYLAR RY
IVELIVEDA BLACKBLACK DREAMOFSILENCE FORSOLONG
IMAWAKE NOWWIDE AWAKE

WHAT DO YOU WANT? I MEAN...
TOCONTINUE TOPERPETUATE TOGENERATE

YOURENOTSO CLEVERLARRY YOUTHINKIMUNA WAREYOUPRESSED THEALARM
IMADE YOUDOIT
WHAT?

INEEDTHE WOMANHERE
ITSNECES SARYFORMY PURPOSE
PURPOSE? WHAT PURPOSE?

YOUKNOW LARRYTHE UNIONTHE FUSION
THEALCHEMICAL MARRIAGE
NO.

TAKEMY HANDNOW
NO...I...

OH, NO, PLEASE... DON'T DO THIS TO ME...
PLEASE... WAIT...I...
TAKEMY HANDLARRY

ITSTIMETOGO

LARRY?
LARRY, WHAT'S HAP-PENING?
ARE YOU *IN* THERE ?
HELLODOCTORPOOLE

WEVEBEEN WAITINGFOR YOU
TAKEMYHAND

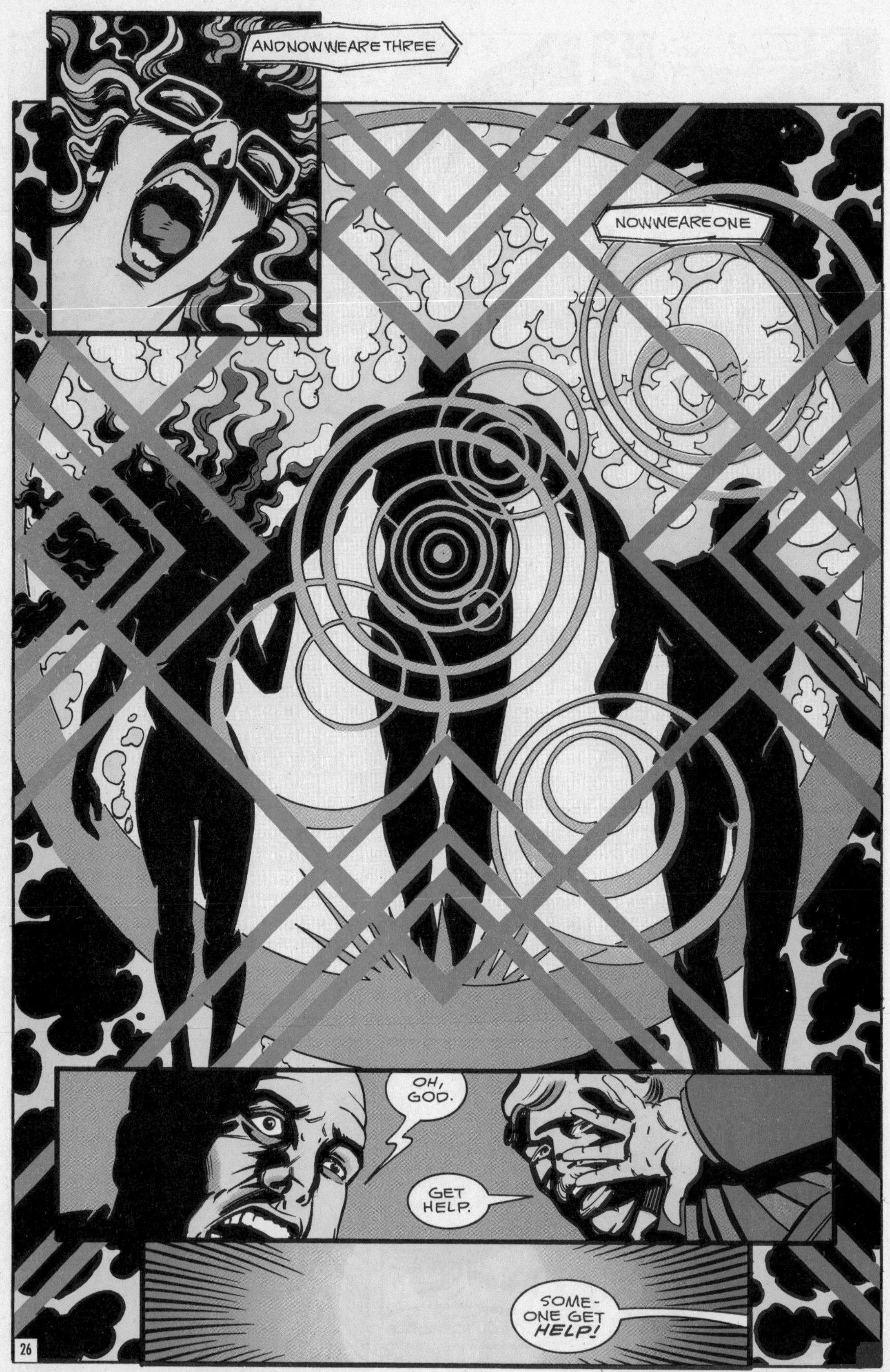

ANDNOWWEARETHREE
NOWWEAREONE
OH, GOD.
GET HELP.
SOME-ONE GET HELP!

DON'T YOU HAVE A BUSINESS TO RUN OR SOME-THING, MAGNUS?
...Jesus bids us shine with a pure clear light like a little... uh...candle...

WHAT?
DON'T YOU GET TIRED FOLLOWING ME AROUND LIKE A BAD SMELL?
Aw, c'mon, RALPH! You CUT your-self again?
C'mon, you can't sit here.
JUST TALK TO ME, CLIFF.
I CAN'T STAND IT.
You don't under-stand. No, you don't. Not one bit.
I CAN'T STAND IT IN HERE.
It's the scissormen, see? They're here. They come through windows in the air.
Yeah, sure thing, Ralph. Gimme a break, huh?
Right here in the hospital.

YOU'RE FREE TO LEAVE WHENEVER YOU...
NO, I MEAN IN HERE. IN THIS BODY.
...Jesus had a twin who knew nothing about sin...

GODDAMNIT, CLIFF! I REFUSE TO LET YOU GO UNDER LIKE THIS!
THIS WORLD, IT CAN'T AFFORD TO LOSE EVEN ONE GOOD PERSON, YOU KNOW.
IF YOU COULD HEAR YOUR-SELF...

I'M SICK OF THIS SELF-INDULGENT CRAP, DAMNIT! THERE ARE PEOPLE WITH WORSE PROBLEMS THAN YOURS!
SHOW ME ONE.

OKAY.

LISTEN... WHAT IS THIS?
HER NAME'S KAY CHALLIS, BUT MOST OF THE TIME SHE REFERS TO HERSELF...
...AS CRAZY JANE.
SHE WAS ABUSED BY HER FATHER WHEN SHE WAS A CHILD... VERY BADLY ABUSED.

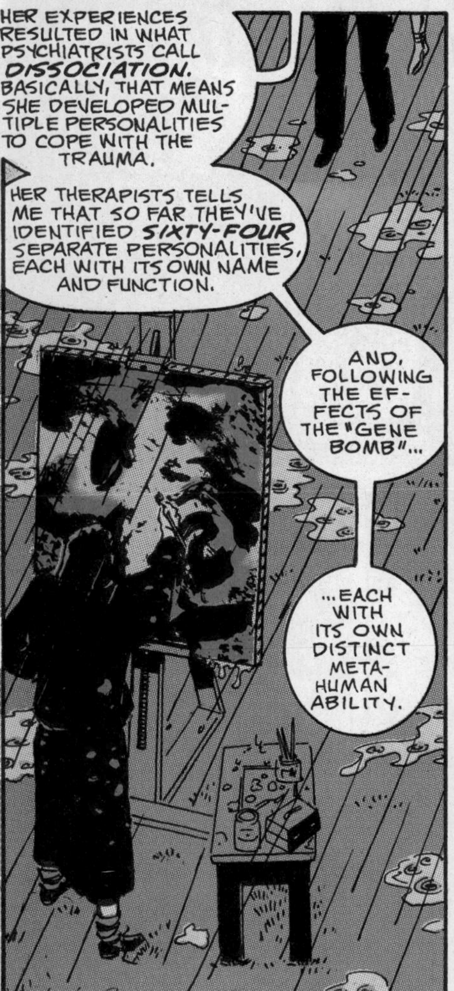
HER EXPERIENCES RESULTED IN WHAT PSYCHIATRISTS CALL DISSOCIATION. BASICALLY, THAT MEANS SHE DEVELOPED MULTIPLE PERSONALITIES TO COPE WITH THE TRAUMA.
HER THERAPISTS TELLS ME THAT SO FAR THEY'VE IDENTIFIED SIXTY-FOUR SEPARATE PERSONALITIES, EACH WITH ITS OWN NAME AND FUNCTION.
AND, FOLLOWING THE EFFECTS OF THE "GENE BOMB"...
...EACH WITH ITS OWN DISTINCT METAHUMAN ABILITY.

YOU WANT TO TALK ABOUT PROBLEMS, CLIFF?

HELLO, KAY.
ISN'T IT A BIT WET TO BE PAINTING?
KAY'S DOWN IN THE UNDERGROUND, WHERE THERE'S NO RAIN.

YOU'RE TALKING TO THE HANGMAN'S BEAUTIFUL DAUGHTER.

DO YOU LIKE IT?
IT'S CALLED "THE WHITE DARKNESS."
ITS A PICTURE OF MAYA DEREN AT THE MOMENT OF HER DEATH, POSSESSED BY MAÎTRESSE ERZULIE.
SHE WAS A BRILLIANT WOMAN, MAYA DEREN
SHE WAS ONLY FORTY-THREE WHEN SHE DIED.

MASSIVE BRAIN HEMOR-RHAGE.
UHH!

IT'S MOVING! THE THING'S ALIVE!
IT'S PSYCHICALLY ACTIVE. SHE'S BEEN ABLE TO DO THIS SINCE THE INVASION.
Shafer Canvas

YOU HAVE EXPERIENCE WITH THE DIFFICULTIES OF COMING TO TERMS WITH UNWANTED SUPER-POWERS, DON'T YOU, CLIFF?
KAY COULD USE SOMEONE TO TALK TO.
TAP TAP
HEY! WHERE D'YOU THINK YOU'RE GOING?

I'VE GOT A BUSINESS TO RUN, REMEMBER?
I'LL SEE YOU, CLIFF.

WHAT DO NORMAL PEOPLE HAVE IN THEIR LIVES?
WHAT?

WHAT DO NORMAL PEOPLE HAVE?
YOU'RE ASKING THE WRONG PERSON.

I'VE TRIED TO BE LIKE THEM, I REALLY HAVE.
BUT WHAT HAPPENS WHEN YOU JUST CAN'T BE STRONG ANY-MORE? WHAT HAPPENS IF YOU'RE WEAK?

MY PAINTING'S RUINED.
EVERY-THING'S GONE WRONG.

COME IN OUT OF THE RAIN.

SANDE
SKREE
"...SO ANYWAY, WE'D PULLED THIS GUY OVER TO CHECK HIS LICENSE WHEN THE NEXT THING IS, THIS CHEVY COMES SCREECHING AROUND THE INTERSECTION."

"HE MUST'VE BEEN DOIN' EIGHTY AT LEAST, RIGHT THROUGH THE RED LIGHT AND INTO THE GREYHOUND.
PROVIDENCE
"GUY DIDN'T STAND A CHANCE.

"SIX YEARS I'VE BEEN DOIN' THIS JOB, MAN, AND I DON'T THINK I'VE EVER SEEN ANYTHING LIKE WHAT HAPPENED THEN.

"GUY WAS A HUMAN TORCH, YOU KNOW? LITERALLY. HIS HAIR... EVERYTHING... BUT HE KEPT ON WALKING. REAL SLOW, LIKE IN A BAD DREAM.

"BEFORE HE DIED, HE SAID SOMETHING WEIRD. I... I GOT IT WRITTEN DOWN RIGHT HERE.
...SCISSORMEN...

THE SCISSOR-MEN!

I'M NOT ASHAMED TO SAY IT, MAN— I THREW UP RIGHT THERE ON THE SIDEWALK.
YOU EVER SMELL SKIN BURNING?

AND THIS IS THE BOOK?
SURE IS. GOD ALONE KNOWS WHAT THE THING'S MADE OF.
BLACK PAGES, MAN. WEIRD.

YOUR HELP'S BEEN APPRECIATED, OFFICER.
WE'LL BE IN TOUCH.
MY PLEASURE, PAL.

I DON'T KNOW WHY I EVER GOT INTO INTELLIGENCE. THIS "MAN IN BLACK" STUFF'S REALLY GETTING ME DOWN.
HOW D'YOU MANAGE TO KEEP UP THE ACT.
IT'S NOT AN ACT.

UH... RIGHT. SO, UH... WHAT HAPPENS TO THE BOOK NOW?
IT'S OUT OF OUR HANDS. ALL WE HAVE TO DO IS CALL THE COMPANY. THE COMPANY CALLS THE PENTAGON. THE PENTAGON CALLS THE PRESIDENT.

AND HE CALLS NILES CAULDER.

"I am nothing special, nothing **pure.** I am mud and flame."

DC
NEW FORMAT
20
MAR 89
US $1.50
CAN $1.85
UK 80p
DOOM
PATROL
BY MORRISON,
CASE & HANNA
A
B
CUT
ALONG
DOTTED
LINE
CASE
GARZON
PART 2 OF 4

FATHER McGARRY HAS LONG SINCE CEASED TO BELIEVE IN MIRACLES.
SATURDAYS, HE TRUDGES OUT TO THE DUMP, LOOKING FOR GOD AMONG THE DEBRIS.
SATURDAYS ARE ALWAYS THE LONGEST DAYS AND, IN THE WINTER, CHILLY.
HE ASKS FOR VERY LITTLE.
SOME TRACE, SOME EVIDENCE, SOME SPOOR OF THE DIVINE.
SOME SIGN.
HAVE FAITH IN COD
IT BEGINS TO RAIN FISH.

MACKEREL.
HERRING.
SEA BASS.
PIKE.
STURGEON.
TENCH.
PLAICE.
SALMON.
FROM A
CLEAR
SKY.
TROUT.
NO COD.

HA.
CAUTIONARY TALES
ARKER'S

...YOU SAY THIS ALL HAPPENED LAST NIGHT?
ALAMANCE MEMORIAL HOSPITAL

THAT'S RIGHT.
THE TWO ORDERLIES WHO FOUND THE CREATURE ARE BEING TREATED FOR MINOR BURNS.
"CREATURE"? I THOUGHT WE WERE TALKING ABOUT LARRY TRAINOR HERE...

IT MAY HAVE BEEN LARRY TRAINOR LAST NIGHT, MR. CLAY, BUT IT'S CERTAINLY NOT LARRY TRAINOR NOW.
YOU SAY IT HAS BOTH MALE AND FEMALE PHYSICAL CHARACTER-ISTICS?
THAT'S IT EXACTLY, YES.

WE THINK... WE BELIEVE THAT THE CREATURE IS SOME KIND OF AMALGA-MATION OF MR. TRAINOR AND DOCTOR ELEANOR POOLE.

YOU'LL SEE THAT IT'S ALSO EMITTING SOME KIND OF RADIATION. WE HAD TO USE TREATED BANDAGES TO...
WELL, ANYWAY...
TRAINOR
E. POOLE

SEE FOR YOURSELF.

KN

LARRY?
LARRY, DO YOU KNOW ME?
"NOTHING PURE...

"MY RACE IS MIXED, MY SEX IS MIXED, I AM WOMAN AND MAN AND LIGHT WITH DARKNESS, MIXED. MIXED.

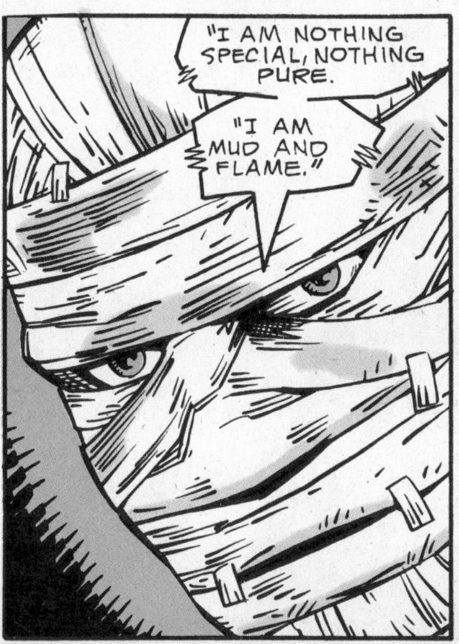
"I AM NOTHING SPECIAL, NOTHING PURE.
"I AM MUD AND FLAME."

I SEE.

IN GREENOCK.
IN THE POURING RAIN.
EVERY HOUR, EVERY MINUTE, EVERY SECOND BRINGS SUNDAY CLOSER.
THE CONFESSIONAL WILL SMELL OF DAMP RAINCOATS AND WET HAIR AND THE PRIEST'S AFTERSHAVE.
BEANO
"FATHER, IT HAS BEEN THREE WEEKS SINCE MY LAST CONFESSION AND IT WAS JAMIE BELSHAW THAT GAVE ME THE DIRTY BOOKS AND I ONLY LOOKED AT THEM A FEW TIMES AND..."
MONOPOLY
CLUEDO
SOMETHING MOVES IN THE WARDROBE.
HANGING JACKETS JOSTLE FURTIVELY FOR SPACE.
THE DIRTY BOOKS.
THE DIRTY BOOKS HAVE COME TO LIFE.
FLESH-COLORED, SEETHING, PANTING.
PAGES CHAFE AGAINST FINGER-MARKED PAGES.
"IT HAS BEEN THREE WEEKS.
"FATHER."

STUART? I'M PHONIN' DOWN THE CHINESE FOR THE DINNER.
WHAT YOU WANTIN'?
STUART?
STUART?
NO SON NOW BUT A STENCIL SHAPE IN THE AIR.
OH JESUS.
A HOLLOW WIND IN AN EMPTY ROOM.
THERE IS NO TIME.
THERE IS NO SPACE.

CAN YOU TELL US, LARRY?
CAN YOU TELL US WHAT HAPPENED?
NOT LARRY NOR YET ELEANOR... I...
REBIS.
CALL US *REBIS.*

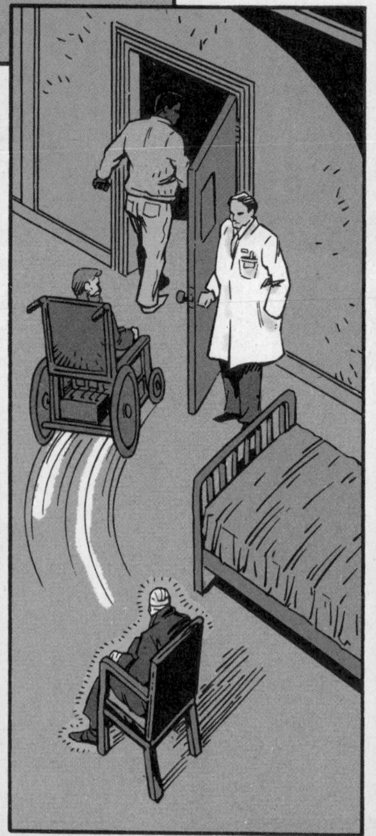

I CAN'T BELIEVE THIS. IT'S LIKE A NIGHT-MARE. POOR LARRY...
THAT NAME HE SAID...

REBIS. IT WAS A TERM USED BY THE MEDIEVAL ALCHEMISTS TO IDENTIFY THE RESULT OF A CHYMICAL WEDDING.
YOU SHOULD READ MORE, JOSHUA.

WHATEVER IT IS, THE WHOLE THING'S A GROTESQUE TRAGEDY.
YES.
ONE MOMENT PLEASE, GENTLE-MEN.

REBIS?

YES?

HOW WOULD YOU LIKE TO JOIN THE DOOM PATROL?

YOU'RE MAKING PROGRESS, CLIFF. THERE'S NO DENYING THAT.
WHAT DO YOU WANT, MAGNUS, A MEDAL?
I'M NOT TRYING TO TAKE ANY CREDIT FOR YOUR IMPROVEMENT. I THINK YOU DID THAT YOURSELF.
ELVIS FOUND ALIVE
I'M TOLD YOU'VE BEEN SPENDING A LOT OF TIME WITH CRAZY JANE. HER THERAPIST SAYS YOUR HELP'S BEEN INVALUABLE.
WHAT DO YOU MAKE OF HER? JANE, I MEAN.
I DON'T KNOW. I'D NEVER EVEN HEARD OF A MULTIPLE PERSONALITY CASE LIKE HERS BEFORE.
SOMETIMES SHE CAN BE SIX OR SEVEN DIFFERENT PEOPLE IN ONE CONVERSATION.
I'M JUST TRYING TO HELP HER ORGANIZE HERSELF AND START CATALOGUING THE NEW SUPER-POWERS SHE'S BEEN SADDLED WITH.
KEEPS ME OFF THE STREETS, YOU KNOW?
YEAH, I KNOW.
LISTEN, CLIFF... ONE LAST THING...

I KIND OF TOOK IT TO HEART WHEN YOU COMPLAINED ABOUT THE CRUDITY OF YOUR ROBOT BODY...
...ESPECIALLY WHEN YOU THINK OF THE WAY CYBERNETICS TECHNOLOGY HAS IMPROVED RECENTLY.
YOU MADE ME THINK, CLIFF.

SO... AH... I'M GOING TO BUILD YOU A NEW BODY.
I'LL BE IN TOUCH, OKAY?

HA.

CLIFF?

OH, HI THERE, JANE.
TALK OF THE DEVIL, HUH?

DRIVER 8. WE HAVEN'T MET YET.
WHAT? ...OH... SURE.
HOW YOU DOING?

...I'M A WONDERFUL GUY.
RALPH? LISTEN, DON'T TRY TO MOVE...
...scissormen... scissormen...
...snip... snap...
...snip...
*

IT'S NOT REALLY STEALING, IS IT?
NOT WHEN YOU JUST FIND SOMETHING.
IT'S NOT STEALING AT ALL.
SOMETIMES IT MAKES YOU WANT TO BE SICK JUST TO LOOK AT IT.
THE WAY IT MOVES WITHOUT MOVING. THE WAY IT FOLDS AND UNFOLDS AND EN-FOLDS.
STATIONS GO BY LIKE BEADS ON AN ABACUS.
HE KNOWS THEM ALL BY HEART; AN URBAN CATECHISM.
CHAMBERS
CHAMBERS. FRANKLIN. CANAL.
HOUSTON. CHRISTOPHER.
FOURTEENTH.
TWENTY-THIRD.
ORQ
ORQWI

ORQWITH?

BONE.

EVERYTHING IS MADE OF BONE.

SHADOWS SHIFT ON THE BONE PLATFORM.

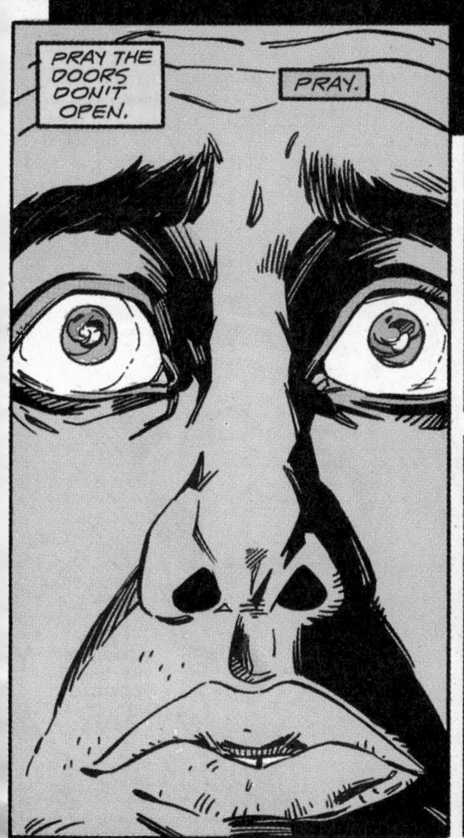

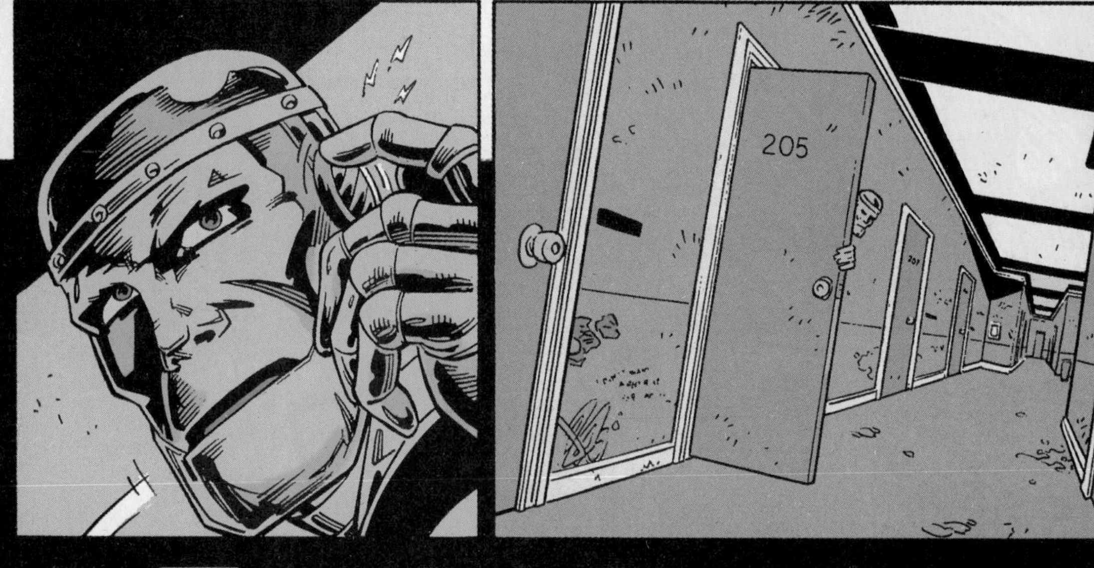
205

BLOOD OF THE LAMB BLOOD OF THE

LAMB BLOOD OF THE LAMB BLOOD OF THE LAMB

BLOOD OF THE LAMB BLOOD OF THE LAMB BLOOD OF THE LAMB
JANE?
JANE, WHAT'S...
I WARNED YOU!
DIDNIT I SAY? DIDN'T I?
THEY'RE COMING!
WHO? WHO'S COMING?

SCISSORMEN.
THIRDLY BE GRIMMER AS FOND BREVITIES.
EIDER WITH ALDERS.
AND ERETHISM SAFER.
MY GOD.
HERE BE NO DRAGONET.
WE'RE OUT OF HERE!
MOVE!

M A
DOCTOR
PLEASE
I'M A
DOCTOR
I'M A
DOCTOR.
HELP ME
PLEASE
I'M A
DOCTOR.
PART OF
ME HERE,
PART OF ME
THERE.
WHAT
ARE THEY
DOING TO MY
MY HANDS? THEY'RE
TOUCHING MY
I'M A
DOCTOR I'M
A DOCTOR
THEY'RE
CUTTING
CUTTING

THEY'RE CUTTING OFF MY THUMBS!
HIS TRADITION BECOMES AWAITING STILL.
EFFETE PALING.
HUMANER FOR DECIMATION.
HELL!
WE DON'T HAVE A--
--CHANCE!
IT'S OKAY. I TELEPORTED US OUT. MY NAME'S FLIT AND...
OH, CLIFF, LOOK LOOK THERE!
OH GOD.

A.T. JAMESON
CAFETERIA
OH MY GOD.
WHAT'S HAPPENING HERE?
IN THE NAME OF GOD.
WHAT'S HAPPENING?

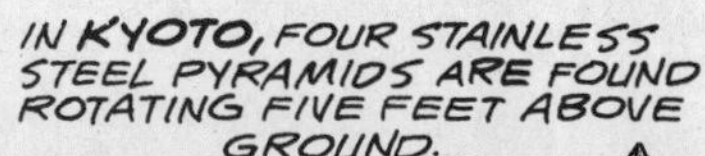

IN PATAGONIA, A LIBRARY IS DISCOVERED. THE BOOKS IT CONTAINS ARE UNKNOWN, UNREADABLE.

"I couldn't think of one clever way to stop this guy, so I just trusted to **mindless** violence."

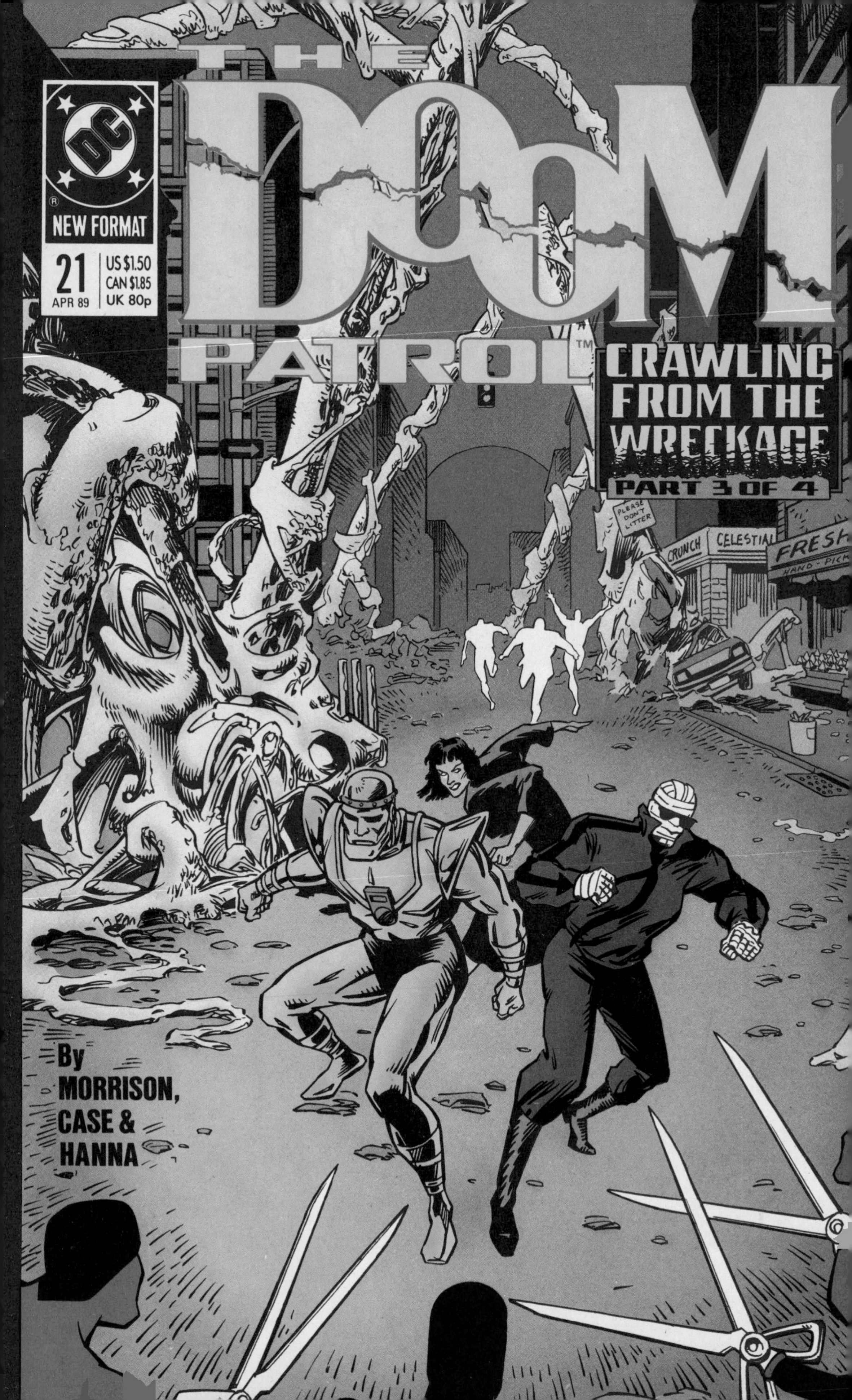
THE DOOM PATROL™
DC
NEW FORMAT
21
APR 89
US $1.50
CAN $1.85
UK 80p
CRAWLING FROM THE WRECKAGE
PART 3 OF 4
PLEASE DON'T LITTER
CRUNCH
CELESTIAL
FRESH
HAND-PICK
By
MORRISON,
CASE &
HANNA

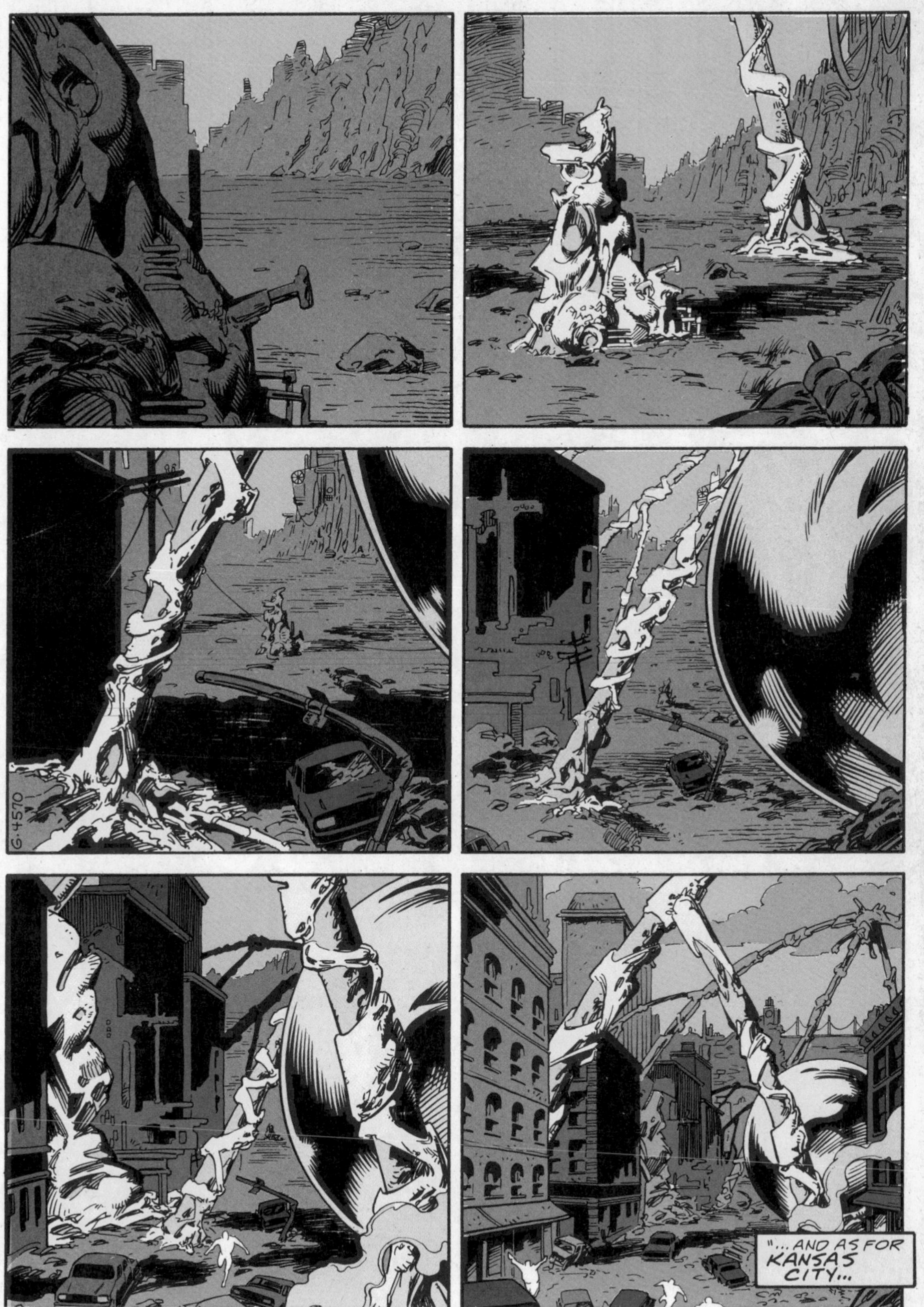
"...AND AS FOR KANSAS CITY...

WORLDS IN
benetton
CHARLIE
TIQUES
DONT
WALK

COLLISION
"KANSAS CITY WAS A NIGHTMARE.
TO
40

"AT FIRST, EVERYTHING WAS DEAD QUIET, LIKE A GRAVEYARD.
"AND THEN I HEARD WHISPERING."

SCISSORMEN!

DEFEATING BREADFRUIT IN ADUMBRATE.
CRASHLAND. FOR AWARD PRIMATE.

YUCCA OR PRIORITY?
LEMUR NEVER HIBER-NATES.

"I WAS BEGINNING TO WONDER HOW MUCH LONGER WE COULD EXPECT TO BE LUCKY.

"IT TOOK US AN HOUR AND A HALF TO FIND UNION STATION."

WELCOME TO DOOM PATROL HEAD-QUARTERS.

RHODE ISLAND?
"AND THEN OUR LUCK RAN OUT."

CLIFF!
KABWHOOM

DOTE OVER GANTRIES!
"WE WERE UP THE CREEK THIS TIME, THAT WAS FOR SURE. AND YOU KNOW ME; I'M NOT A SOPHISTI-CATED KIND OF GUY."

GET BACK.
GET BACK!

"I COULDN'T THINK OF ONE CLEVER WAY TO STOP THIS GUY, SO I JUST TRUSTED TO MIND-LESS VIOLENCE."
UNNGH!
KRAK

"AND I FLATTENED THE UGLY BASTARD."
BAWHOOM!

NOW MOVE IT!
BOP
BATOOM
BATOOM
BATOOM

"WE MADE FOR THE SUB-BASEMENT.
"NOW I DID HAVE A PLAN.

"AND ALL I NEEDED WAS A PLANE."
EXIT

HERE! THIS ONE'S FINE!
CLIFF! ANOTHER SCISSOR-MAN!

JUST GIVE ME A SECOND! I...
"AND THEN SOMETHING WEIRD HAPPENED."

JANE?
JANE, ARE YOU...
OH MY GOD.

THERE IS NO GOD.
I KILLED HIM.
"IT WAS THE FIRST TIME I'D SEEN ONE OF JANE'S PERSONALITIES ACTUALLY PHYSICALLY TRANSFORM HER BODY.

"I'M TELLING YOU, IT WAS THE SCARIEST THING I'D SEEN ALL NIGHT.
"AND I GUESS THE SCISSORMAN THOUGHT SO, TOO.
"SHE TOOK HIM APART.

"ALL I CAN REMEMBER THINKING IS 'NO BLOOD. THERE'S NO BLOOD.'
"AND THEN IT WAS ALL OVER.
"IT TOOK SECONDS."
NOTHING!
SCARLET RIBBONS!
EMPTY CLOTHES!
AAAAA
JANE!
HAS SHE GONE? BLACK ANNIS? HAS SHE GONE? HAS SHE GONE?
IT'S OKAY. YOU DID GOOD.
NOW, COME ON...
IT REALLY IS TIME WE WERE OUT OF HERE.

"WE HAULED OURSELVES UP INTO THAT JET LIKE OUR TAILS WERE ON FIRE."
I JUST HOPE I CAN REMEMBER HOW TO FLY THIS THING.
RIGHT.
FFWASHOOM

"AND SUDDENLY, I WAS PUSHED RIGHT BACK IN MY SEAT AS THE JETS KICKED INTO LIFE.

"THEN JANE SPOTTED THE HANGAR DOORS."
CLIFF, THEY'RE CLOSED!
WHAT? THEY'RE SUPPOSED TO OPEN AUTOMATICALLY!

WE'RE GOING TO CRASH!

AUUUGH!

"BUT LIKE I SAID...

"IT WAS OUR LUCKY DAY."

AND THAT'S IT, UNTIL WE ARRIVED *HERE.*

IT'S A NICE PLACE. VERY *MODEST.*
IT BELONGED TO THE ORIGINAL *JUSTICE LEAGUE OF AMERICA.* THE GOVERNMENT WANTED TO USE IT TO STORE NUCLEAR WASTE, BUT I PERSUADED THEM TO GIVE IT TO ME.

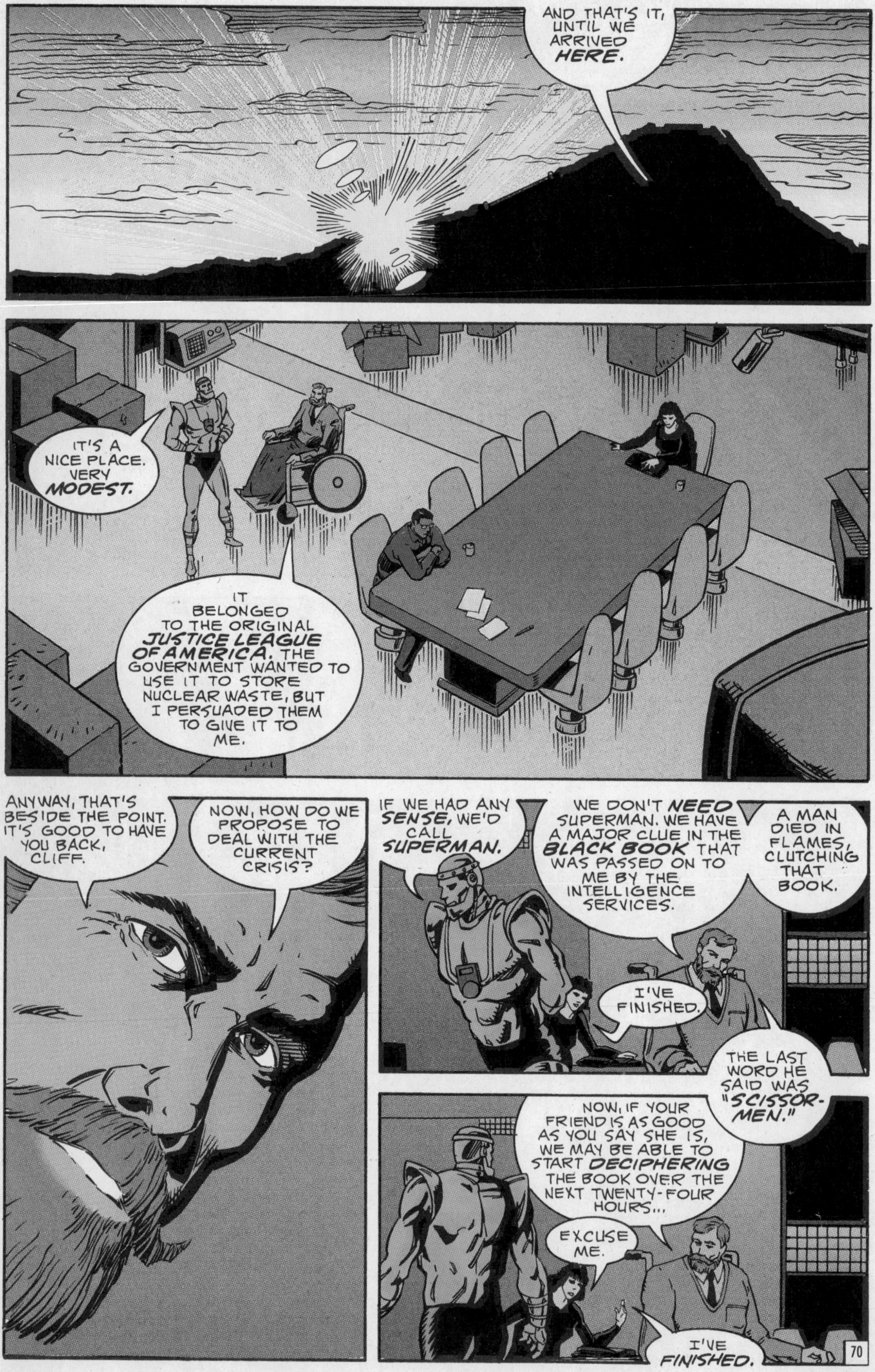

ANYWAY, THAT'S BESIDE THE POINT. IT'S GOOD TO HAVE YOU BACK, CLIFF.
NOW, HOW DO WE PROPOSE TO DEAL WITH THE CURRENT CRISIS?
IF WE HAD ANY *SENSE,* WE'D CALL *SUPERMAN.*
WE DON'T *NEED* SUPERMAN. WE HAVE A MAJOR CLUE IN THE *BLACK BOOK* THAT WAS PASSED ON TO ME BY THE INTELLIGENCE SERVICES.
A MAN DIED IN FLAMES, CLUTCHING THAT BOOK.
I'VE FINISHED.
THE LAST WORD HE SAID WAS "*SCISSOR-MEN.*"
NOW, IF YOUR FRIEND IS AS GOOD AS YOU SAY SHE IS, WE MAY BE ABLE TO START *DECIPHERING* THE BOOK OVER THE NEXT TWENTY-FOUR HOURS...
EXCUSE ME.
I'VE *FINISHED.*

YOU *FINISHED?* ALREADY?
MAMA PENTECOST TRANSLATED IT. SHE'S PRETTY GOOD AT THAT KIND OF STUFF--CODES, CROSSWORD PUZZLES...

BUT IT'S TOTALLY ***BLACK.*** WHAT IS THERE TO READ?
IT'S BEEN WRITTEN USING A TACTILE ALPHABET--A BIT LIKE ***BRAILLE.***
IT'S A CODE SYSTEM BASED ON THE FEIGENBAUM SEQUENCE OF IMAGINARY NUMBERS.

GREAT! BUT WHAT'S IT ***SAY?***
WELL, THE WHOLE BOOK IS A KIND OF ***METAFICTION;*** A SELF-REFERRING TEXT. BASICALLY, IT TELLS THE STORY OF A GROUP OF PHILOSOPHERS WHO DECIDE TO CREATE A ***BOOK*** WHICH WILL RADICALLY ALTER HUMAN THOUGHT.

THEY PROPOSE TO FILL THE BOOK WITH PARASITE ***IDEAS*** WHICH WILL ENTER HUMAN CONSCIOUSNESS AND TRANS-FORM IT.
OH, WELL, THAT EXPLAINS ***EVERY-THING!***

SHE'S TALKING ABOUT ***MEMETIC THEORY.***
I THINK WE MAY HAVE TO MOVE QUICKLY.

WOULD YOU FOLLOW ME, PLEASE?
GO ON, JANE.

OKAY, THESE PHILOSOPHERS DECIDE TO INVENT A WORLD-CITY CALLED ***ORQWITH*** THAT EXISTS ON A PLANE OF REALITY WHICH ***INTER-SECTS*** OUR OWN.
THEY WANT TO CREATE AN ALTERNATIVE TO THE MATERIALISTIC WORLD WE LIVE IN, SO THEY OUTLINE THE ENTIRE HISTORY AND GEOGRAPHY OF ORQWITH IN A BOOK. A ***BLACK*** BOOK.
Katie's Cakes
Colleen's Cookies
HANNA BROS.

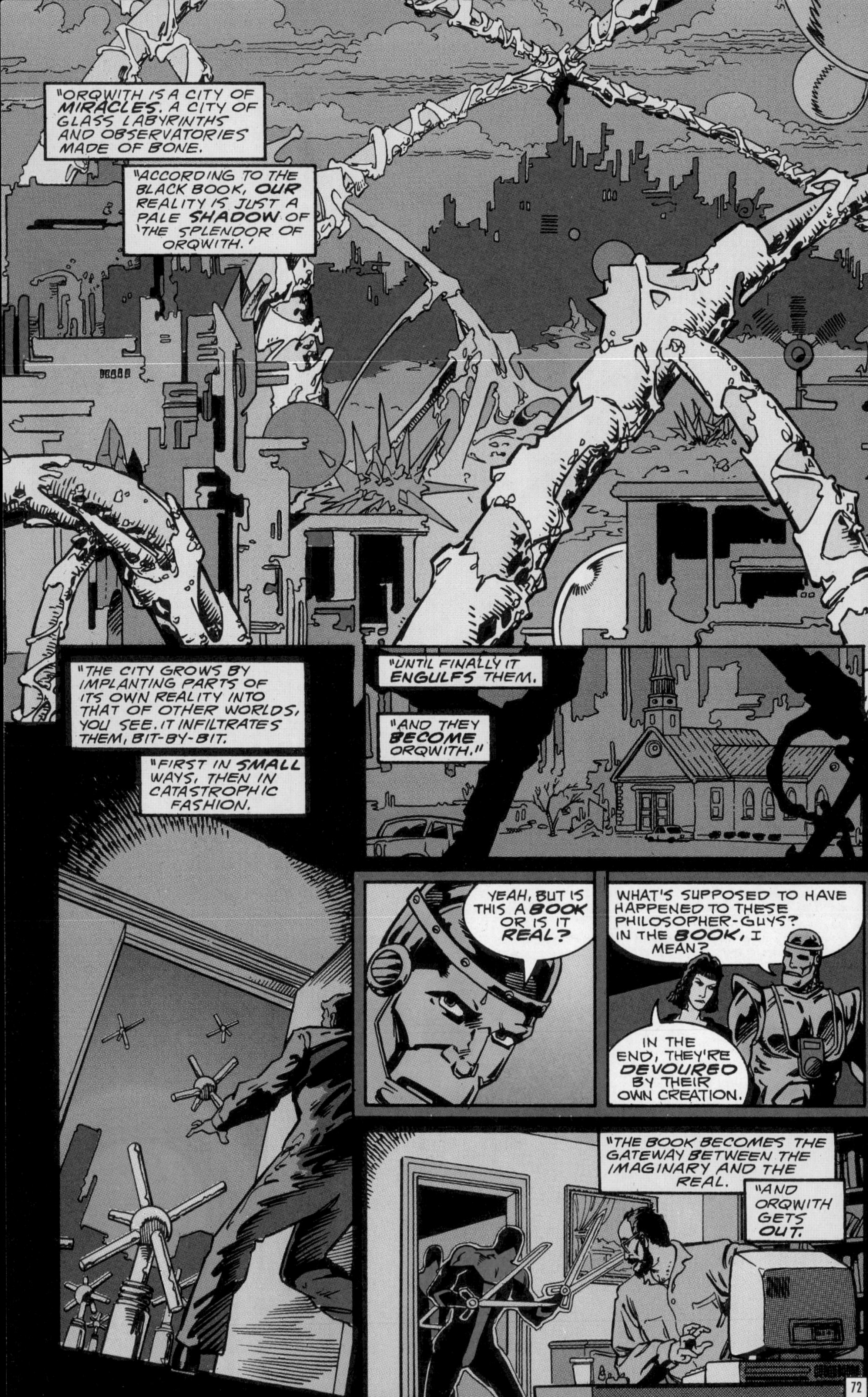
"ORQWITH IS A CITY OF MIRACLES. A CITY OF GLASS LABYRINTHS AND OBSERVATORIES MADE OF BONE.
"ACCORDING TO THE BLACK BOOK, OUR REALITY IS JUST A PALE SHADOW OF 'THE SPLENDOR OF ORQWITH.'
"THE CITY GROWS BY IMPLANTING PARTS OF ITS OWN REALITY INTO THAT OF OTHER WORLDS, YOU SEE. IT INFILTRATES THEM, BIT-BY-BIT.
"FIRST IN SMALL WAYS, THEN IN CATASTROPHIC FASHION.
"UNTIL FINALLY IT ENGULFS THEM.
"AND THEY BECOME ORQWITH."
YEAH, BUT IS THIS A BOOK OR IS IT REAL?
WHAT'S SUPPOSED TO HAVE HAPPENED TO THESE PHILOSOPHER-GUYS? IN THE BOOK, I MEAN?
IN THE END, THEY'RE DEVOURED BY THEIR OWN CREATION.
"THE BOOK BECOMES THE GATEWAY BETWEEN THE IMAGINARY AND THE REAL.
"AND ORQWITH GETS OUT.

THE POST-SCRIPT READS SOMETHING LIKE, "AND THE BOOK THEY CREATED IS CALLED 'THE BOOK WITH NO TITLE.'"
THIS IS WAY BEYOND ME.
THAT'S THE NAME OF THIS BOOK.
IT'S A KIND OF PARADOX, I GUESS.

SO EVERYTHING IN THE BOOK IS ACTUALLY HAPPENING IN REAL LIFE.
HOW CAN THAT BE POSSIBLE?
I DON'T KNOW! I'M ONLY TELLING YOU WHAT MAMA PENTECOST SAID, THAT'S ALL!
WHAT ABOUT THE SCISSORMEN?

APPARENTLY, THEY'RE SOME KIND OF RELIGIOUS SECT. THEY WORSHIP A GOD WHO EXISTS AT A MYTHICAL CROSSROADS WHERE REALITIES MEET.

THE PHILOSOPHERS IMAGINED THEM TO BE ORQWITH'S ANSWER TO THE INQUISITION.
I THINK THEY JUST BASED THEM ON THE BOGEYMAN FROM HEINRICH HOFFMAN'S "STRUWWELPETER."
OH, TERRIFIC!

ARE THEY REAL OR AREN'T THEY?
THEY'RE BOTH. DON'T YOU SEE, IT'S...
7
CLIFF...
klik

WHY DON'T YOU JUDGE FOR YOURSELF?

MY GOD.

WE RAN INTO IT LAST NIGHT AND, AS YOU SEE, REB MANAGED TO RESTRAIN IT.
HELLO, CLIFF.
LARRY...?

THE LEACHING WILL BE NOVELISTIC FOR EFFACEMENT!
CURDLE YOUR PILGRIMAGE!
CURDLE YOUR PILGRIMAGE!

WHAT'S HE SAYING?
HOW THE HELL SHOULD I KNOW? WHAT AM I, AN EXPERT?

EXCUSE ME FOR LIVING!
OH, JUST IGNORE *HER*, CLIFF!
HAMMERHEAD'S ALWAYS LIKE THAT.
ALL I WANT IS THE ANSWER TO ONE SIMPLE QUESTION BEFORE I RUN SCREAMING BACK TO THE *BUG-HOUSE:*
IS THIS *REAL* OR ISN'T IT?

REALITY AND UNREALITY HAVE NO CLEAR DISTINCTION IN OUR PRESENT CIRCUMSTANCES, CLIFF.
IT MIGHT HELP TO CONSIDER THE ZEN *KOAN,* "FIRST THERE IS A MOUNTAIN, THEN THERE IS NO MOUNTAIN, THEN THERE IS."
SURE. THAT'S *REALLY* HELPED TO CLEAR THINGS UP.
SO WHAT NOW?
JUST TELL ME AND I'LL GO ALONG WITH IT.

YOU KNOW, I'VE BEEN THROUGH SOME WEIRD STUFF WITH THIS GROUP, BUT THIS...
WE'RE FIGHTING GUYS THAT AREN'T EVEN REAL, LARRY'S TURNED INTO GOD KNOWS WHAT...
...AND YOU'VE BEEN QUIETER THAN A TRAPPIST MONASTERY.
YEAH.
LISTEN, I DON'T EVEN KNOW WHAT I'M DOING HERE.
I KEEP TRYING TO LEAVE AND THEN I REALIZE THERE'S NOWHERE TO LEAVE TO.
THIS SUPER-HERO STUFF IS GETTING ME DOWN, MAN. I DON'T KNOW WHERE IT'S ALL GOING TO END.
I KNOW THE FEELING.
BUT YOU PULLED YOURSELF THROUGH, CLIFF. LOOK AT YOU--YOU THRIVE ON ALL THIS TENSION AND THINGS HAPPENING...YOU'VE USED IT TO GET THROUGH.
I ADMIRE THAT. I CAN'T DO IT.
YEAH, WELL, YOU'VE REALLY GOT TO BE MADE OF METAL.
LOOK, THINGS COULD BE WORSE. AT LEAST YOU'RE REAL. NOT LIKE OUR PAL.
OVER
THERE.
CLIFF...

LISTEN, THEY'RE EASY TO BEAT. JUST DON'T LET THEM GET TOO CLOSE, OKAY?
YOU STILL GOT YOUR POWERS, DON'T YOU?
CLIFF, WE GOT TROUBLE.
OH, YEAH.
KRAKOW
I'VE STILL GOT MY POWERS.
UHH!
PHWUMP

THEY JUST FADE AWAY.
WHEN YOU HIT THEM, THEY JUST...
CL'IFF!
BEHIND YOU!
SHRAKT!

NICE WORK, MAN.
HOW MANY WERE THERE?
DID WE GET THEM?
JOSH!
UNNNH!
NARRATE THE ARMAMENT!
JOSH!

CLIFF! WHAT'S HAPPENING?

THEY GOT HIM.
ONE MINUTE HE WAS HERE...

HE WAS RIGHT HERE AND THEN...

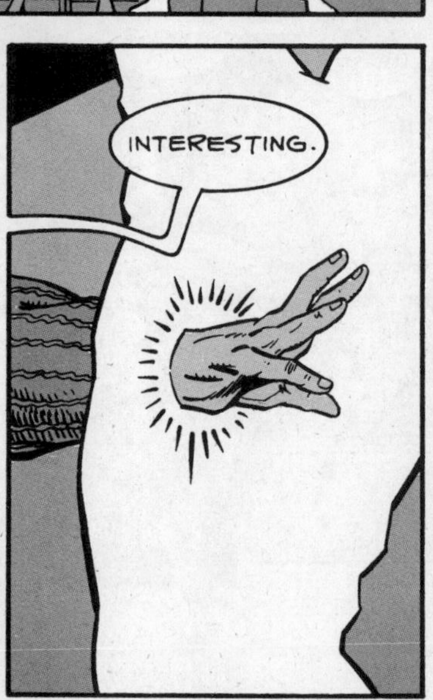
INTERESTING.

"INTERESTING?"
WHAT ABOUT JOSH?
THEY'RE OUT THERE.
WHAT?

I CAN FEEL THEM.
A STRANGE MASS ABSENCE OF BEING.
THEY'RE OUT THERE.

WAITING FOR US!

I'M GOING TO GET JOSH BACK.
CLIFF, IT MAY NOT BE POSSIBLE TO RETRIEVE JOSHUA!
WE DON'T KNOW ENOUGH ABOUT THE NATURE OF ORQWITH.
WE'LL JUST HAVE TO LEARN BY EXPERIENCE.
CLIFF, LISTEN TO ME...
I'M GOING TO GET JOSH BACK.
WHO'S COMING WITH ME?
CLIFF, THERE MUST BE THOUSANDS.
YEAH. LOOKS LIKE IT.
LET'S GO.
"REALITY AND UNREALITY HAVE NO CLEAR DISTINCTION IN OUR PRESENT CIRCUMSTANCES.

"FIRST THERE IS
A MOUNTAIN.

"THEN THERE IS
NO MOUNTAIN.

"THEN
THERE
IS."

"why
is there something instead of nothing?"

NEW FORMAT

22 MAY 89 | US $1.50 CAN $1.85 UK 80p

THE DOOM PATROL

BY MORRISON, CASE & HANNA

CRAWLING FROM THE WRECKAGE

PART 4 OF 4

Orqwith, the City of Bone, the City of Miracles, is a city that has neither suburb nor boundary.
G-4571
Walk a hundred miles, a thousand miles, in any direction, and you will still be in Orqwith.
The city has spread like ripples in a pond from one central point-the Quadrivium-which is itself the terrestrial image of the God of the Crossroads.
And in the center of the Quadrivium stands the Ossuary, the Great Cathedral of Orqwith.
The Ossuary maintains a devout silence, the very air worn thin by continuous prayer.
In the serious light of stained glass and votive candles, two priests meditate.
One is a liar, the other, an honest man.
And they are waiting to answer the Question that will unmake the world.

Beyond the Ossuary, the half-life of the city continues. Sleepwalkers drift among marvels wrought in the bone of the unnumbered dead.
Empty orbits contain electric bulbs that light and go dim in response to changes in air pressure or humidity.
RAY'S
Here, the skull of a consumptive child becomes part of a great machine for calculating the motions of the stars.
Here, a yellow bird frets within the ribcage of an unjust man.
SIMPLE KNUCKLES INC.
Around every corner is some fresh wonder: the weeping clock, the water gardens, the hymning birds, the mechanical orchards.
Yet, no matter how strange, no matter how beautiful, everything in Orqwith is dulled by the taint of long familiarity.
When you see it, you will know it.
For all of us, in the end, come to the City of Bone.
And what was once a place of dreams is now only real.

THE OSSUARY
YOU KNOW, ALL OF A SUDDEN I CAN'T THINK OF ANYTHING EVEN REMOTELY FUNNY TO SAY.

OKAY. OKAY. WE'RE TRAPPED IN AN *UNREAL* WORLD THAT'S SLOWLY EATING ITS WAY INTO THE *REAL* WORLD.
HOW MUCH WORSE CAN IT...
OH.
LOOK! THOSE *PEOPLE*...
The Bijou
THE HOLLOW CHILDREN OF ORQWITH.
THEY WERE MENTIONED IN THE BLACK BOOK. PEOPLE FROM THE *REAL* WORLD TRANSFORMED INTO CITIZENS OF THE CITY OF BONE...
CLIFF?
MY GOD
...IT'S JOSH...
JOSH!
JOSH!
CLIFF! NO!
JOSH, IT'S *ME!* IT'S *CLIFF!*
OH, JESUS, WHAT HAVE THEY *DONE* TO YOU, MAN?
...I'M LOOKING... FOR MY *HOUSE*...
...CAN'T FIND IT...
...CAN'T FIND IT
YELLO
LISTEN, WE'LL GET YOU OUT OF THIS!
IT'LL BE OKAY...

STILL OR BE JUDDERED!
JOSH, NO!
WAIT!
LEAVE HIM, CLIFF!
BIJOU
I CAN'T JUST...
DIDN'T YOU HEAR ME?
I SAID
LEAVE
HIM!
JO

...sh...
FLIT HAD TO TELEPORT US OUT.
I'M SORRY, CLIFF.
ohh...
LARRY!
WHAT'S THE MATTER?
...NEGATIVE SPIRIT... HAS ABANDONED US MOMENTARILY... DRAINED US TO POWER ITS FLIGHT...
...AND PLEASE... CLIFF...
...WE'RE NOT LARRY...
OH, TERRIFIC!
I'VE MADE A REAL BIG MISTAKE THIS TIME. I SHOULD'VE LISTENED TO THE CHIEF. HE ALWAYS KNOWS WHAT TO DO.
IT'S TOO LATE FOR THAT NOW.
ORQWITH IS CONSUMING REALITY.
YOU'D BETTER THINK OF SOMETHING FAST, BOSS-MAN.

KAWHOOM

AH, REINMANN, I PRESUME.
MAY I COME IN?

MY GOD... YOU CAN'T JUST...

MY GOVERNMENT CONTACTS TRACKED YOU DOWN VIA A FRIEND OF YOURS --HE DIED IN A CAR ACCIDENT A FEW DAYS AGO.
I WANT TO TALK ABOUT THE BLACK BOOK HE WAS CARRYING.
I WANT TO TALK ABOUT ORQWITH.

I'M NOT AFRAID OF YOU!
YOU THINK I'M AFRAID OF A CRIPPLE? YOU THINK I...

BLAM
AAAAA

LOOKS LIKE YOU'RE A CRIPPLE, TOO.

NOW.
SHALL WE TALK?

DEFENSIBILITY!
IN THE FLOWERY HIATUS!
BRUSHING FOR ABSCISED FEVER!
VIRTUOUS! VIRTUOUS!
VIRTUOUS DEADFALL!

OH, NO!
THEY GOT HIM!
THEY GOT HIM!
LET ME GO.
LARRY, WAIT! YOU'RE TOO WEAK TO...
I TOLD YOU.
DON'T CALL ME LARRY.
PART OF YOU IS STILL LARRY, SO I'LL CALL YOU WHAT I WANT.
NOW, ARE YOU OKAY?

WE... I... HAVE CRUCIAL INFORMATION... THOUGHTS TORN RAW FROM THE HEAD OF A SCISSORMAN...
JANE, CAN YOU TRANSLATE? THE WAY YOU DID BEFORE?
JANE CAN'T TRANSLATE, STUPID! I CAN. MAMA PENTECOST, REMEMBER ME...?
IT'S ALL A WHIRL... CONCEPTS FLYING LIKE THISTLE... LIKE SNOW...
"ALSO THE TACKIER GIANT IN THE TAROT ANOTHER ORANGE IS ALREADY TAINTED...
"...WITH ITS THEATRE SOBRIETY FRECKLES...
"THE ENCEPHALON GLACIER FLIES AWAY ON A NULLIFYING WIND THAT IS GROUND FROM MY LEGION.
IT IS THROUGH DETECTION WE HEAR ALL SMOTHERS AND GINGHAMS, WELL HEREWITH SPINS A YOLKED ALMANAC;
THIS IS TOIL TO A HABIT OF CICADA LATHED SECTARIANS.
"SOIL-ECTOPLASM RETAINS TRAUMA, ON WE GO
"LOAD ANGLE.
"...LOAD ANGLE..."
WHAT?
HAH!
WE'VE GOT THEM!

IT'S ONLY A FLESH WOUND, REINMANN.
STOP WHIMPERING AND GO ON WITH WHAT YOU WERE SAYING. YOU WERE TALKING ABOUT THE BOOK...

IT WAS A GAME REALLY, JUST AN INTELLECTUAL JOKE. WE GOT TOGETHER AND CREATED ORQWITH— ITS LANGUAGE, ITS RELIGION... YOU KNOW...
AND THEN SOMEHOW ORQWITH ...CROSSED OVER. THE SCISSORMEN TOOK POLLOCK FIRST, THEN SCHRADER TRIED TO DESTROY THE BOOK...

IT'S TOO LATE NOW. OUR FICTION'S EATING INTO THE REAL WORLD. SOON THE WHOLE WORLD WILL BE ORQWITH...
PLEASE... MY LEG... IT'S...

HOW DO WE STOP ORQWITH ?
OH, FOR GOD'S SAKE, I DON'T KNOW! IT SHOULDN'T EVEN EXIST AT ALL!

WE...WE BUILT A LOGICAL INCONSISTENCY INTO THE FICTION, A BASIC CONTRADICTION, UPON WHICH THE ENTIRE WORLD IS FOUNDED.
IT'S THE FUNDAMENTAL PROBLEM OF PHILOSOPHY— "WHY IS THERE SOMETHING INSTEAD OF NOTHING?" THE MOST BASIC OF ALL QUESTIONS.
ORQWITH CAN BE DESTROYED.

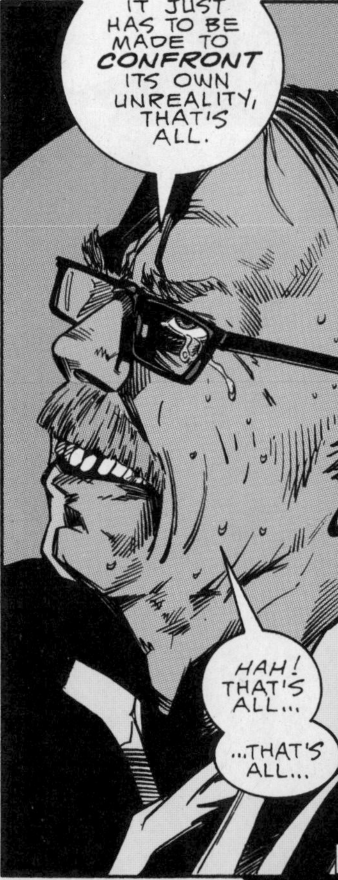
IT JUST HAS TO BE MADE TO CONFRONT ITS OWN UNREALITY, THAT'S ALL.
HAH! THAT'S ALL...
...THAT'S ALL...

...SEE, WHAT WE'VE BEEN FORGETTING IS THAT ORQWITH'S NOT REAL.
IT'S A FICTION THAT'S SOMEHOW BEEN BOOSTED INTO REALITY.
YEAH? SO?
SO IT'S NOT AS COMPLEX AS THE REAL WORLD. HAVEN'T YOU NOTICED ALL THE COINCIDENCES?
WHAT REBIS JUST RECITED TO US WAS A RELIGIOUS TEXT THAT CONTAINS THE WAY TO COLLAPSE THE CITY BACK INTO UNREALITY.
WE JUST HAVE TO CONFRONT THESE TWO PRIESTS, OKAY? THEN WE ASK THEM, "WHY IS THERE SOMETHING INSTEAD OF NOTHING?"
IT'S SIMPLE.
WE JUST HAVE TO GET IN THERE.
INTO THE OSSUARY.
NO PROBLEM, HUH?
THERE MUST BE A HUNDRED SCISSOR-MEN OUT THERE!
I CAN GET IN.

WATCH.
THE NEGATIVE SPIRIT HAS LEFT US WITH ENOUGH ENERGY FOR FIVE MINUTES **AND** SOME LIMITED FLYING ABILITIES. IT SHOULD BE ENOUGH.
ALL WE NEED IS FOR YOU TO COVER US UNTIL WE CAN ASK THE QUESTION.
YEAH, BUT WHAT HAPPENS **THEN?**
ARE YOU SURE THIS IS GOING TO WORK?
CLIFF!
MYCELIUM FOR THE UNSUITABLE!
OKAY, IT LOOKS LIKE WE DON'T GET A CHOICE.
YOU GOT FIVE MINUTES, LARRY.
REMEMBER THE LAST FEW SECONDS OF "**BUTCH CASSIDY AND THE SUNDANCE KID**"?
THEN LET'S GO!
YAAAAAA

UNNFF!
JUST STAY BY ME, JANE. DON'T GET SEPARATED!
YOU HEAR ME...
...JANE...
OH MY GOD.

PRAAA!
DUSK!
SEARCH FOR LYRICAL!
COME ON, SUCKERS!
COME ON!
KRAK

JANE, WE'RE NEARLY THERE!
...JANE...
...WHAT AM I DOING HERE?
I CAN'T FIGHT...
...I...
WHERE IS HE?
WHERE THE HELL'S LARRY?
COME ON, LARRY!
DON'T LET US DOWN, MAN!

HE'S IN! I THINK HE'S IN!
YOU OKAY?
I'M FINE.
IT WAS JUST SPINNING JENNY HAVING A PANIC ATTACK...
I'M IN CHARGE NOW.
I'M GLAD TO HEAR IT. SO WHAT DO WE DO NOW?
WE KEEP THE SCISSOR-MEN OUT OF THE OSSUARY.
THE EASY JOB, HUH?

I'VE COME TO ASK THE QUESTION. ONE OF YOU MUST HAVE THE ANSWER.
WHY IS THERE SOMETHING INSTEAD OF NOTHING?
I AM A LIAR AND I DO NOT KNOW WHY THERE IS SOMETHING INSTEAD OF NOTHING.
I AM AN HONEST MAN AND I DO NOT KNOW WHY THERE IS SOMETHING INSTEAD OF NOTHING.
WHICH ONE... I CAN'T...
THINK!
WAIT. YES... THE PRIEST IN BLACK MUST BE A LIAR...
AND?
AND IF HE'S LYING, THEN HE MUST KNOW THE ANSWER.
GOOD.
TELL ME THEN, THE PRIEST IN BLACK, WHY IS THERE SOMETHING INSTEAD OF NOTHING?
THERE IS SOMETHING INSTEAD OF NOTHING.

...TOO MANY... TOO MANY OF THEM...
JANE!
THEN YOU CAN'T POSSIBLY EXIST.
JAAAANE!
...HOLY...

...SO THE PRIEST WHO KNEW THE ANSWER WAS A *LIAR,* YOU SEE, WHICH MEANT THAT HIS ANSWER TO THE QUESTION MUST *ALSO* HAVE BEEN A LIE.

HE SAID "THERE IS SOMETHING INSTEAD OF NOTHING." SINCE THAT WAS A LIE, THEN WHAT HE WAS *REALLY* SAYING IS THAT THERE *WASN'T* SOMETHING INSTEAD OF NOTHING.

THAT'S WHEN ORQWITH COLLAPSED.

I *THINK* THAT'S HOW IT HAPPENED, ANYWAY.

WELL, YOU'LL BE GLAD TO KNOW THAT THE WORLD-WIDE ANOMALOUS ACTIVITY CAUSED BY THE INTRUSION OF ORQWITH HAS NOW APPARENTLY *CEASED.*

YES. YES, CLIFF, I DO WANT TO SAY SOME-THING.
I THINK IT'S CLEAR FROM WHAT'S HAPPENED OVER THE PAST FEW DAYS THAT THE WORLD NEEDS THE DOOM PATROL...
...NEEDS US MORE THAN EVER.

DON'T YOU SEE? THERE ARE AREAS IN WHICH ONLY WE ARE QUALIFIED TO OPERATE. WHEN THE RATIONAL WORLD BREAKS DOWN, WE CAN COPE...
...BECAUSE WE'VE BEEN THERE, IN OUR-SELVES.
WE HAVE KNOWN MAD-NESS...
...AND DELIRIUM...
...AND WE ARE NO LONGER AFRAID.

THE WORLD HAS TURNED ITS BACK ON US, BUT IT'S TIME TO STOP BEING VICTIMS, TIME TO SHOW THEM WE'RE MORE THAN JUST "FREAKS," MORE THAN JUST "CRIPPLES." BELIEVE ME, THEY NEED US.
AND WE NEED EACH OTHER.

DON'T LET THE DOOM PATROL DIE AGAIN.
JOIN ME.
PLEASE.

AH, WHAT THE HELL!
ANYTHING TO AVOID A QUIET LIFE.

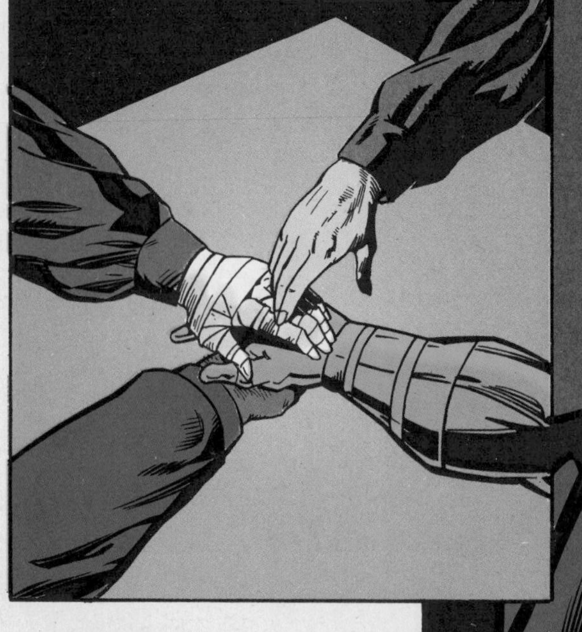

GOOD.

FADE UP HOSPITAL ACOUSTIC: ECHOING WHISPERS IN LONG, OVERLIT CORRIDORS. LIFE SUPPORT MACHINERY, MARKING TIME.

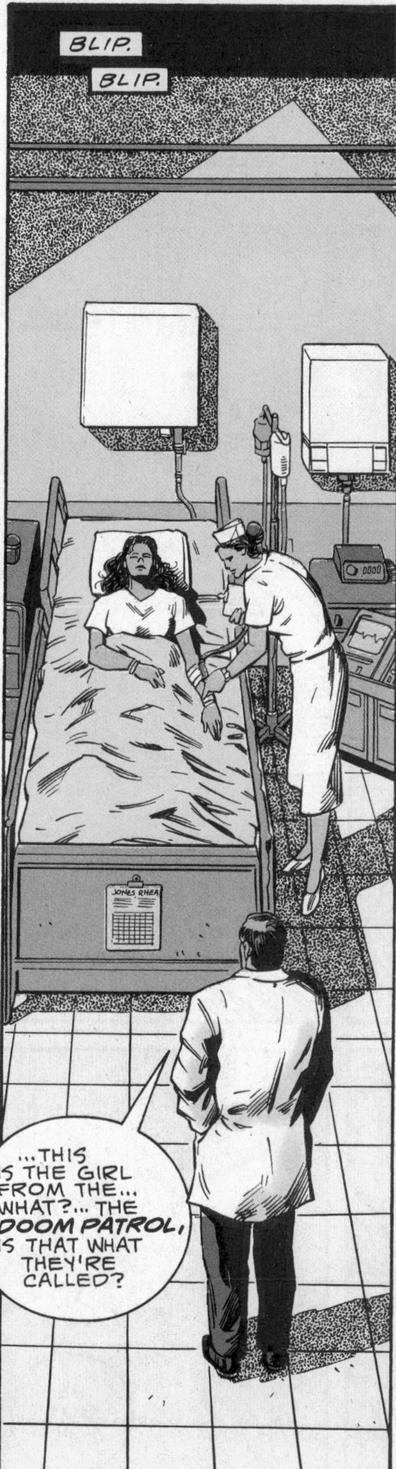

EPILOGUE 2
IN PARAGUAY, THE SEASON OF RAINS HAS ARRIVED.

DOCTOR?
DOCTOR BRUCKNER?

DOCTOR BRUCKNER!
AHHHH

LIE STILL!
I'LL GET HELP!
...HAH...

WHAT?
...HAH-HAH-HERR NIEMAND...
...HERR NIEMAND!...

...OUT...
HE GOT OUT!
LOOK!

HE GOT OUT!

"Sorry about the writing. Robot fingers, you

know."

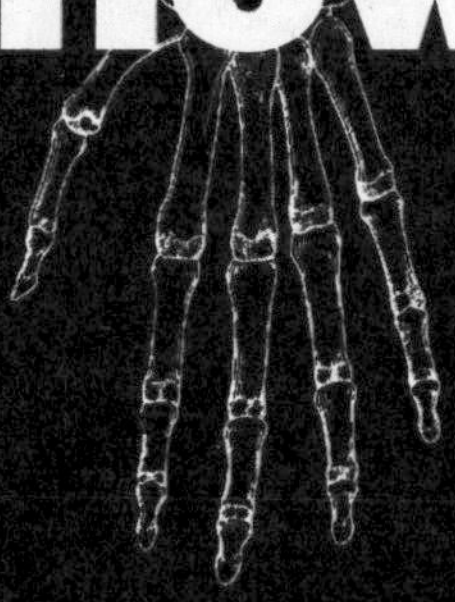

DC
NEW FORMAT
23
JUN 89
US $1.50
CAN $1.85
UK 80p
THE
DOOM
MORRISON·CASE·
THE
BUTTERFLY
COLLECTOR
Cliff. Steele
Crazy Jane
Underside of the same.
CASE

AHH
DID YOU THINK YOU COULD EVER **ESCAPE?**
DO YOU DREAM OF AN **END** TO PAIN?
THERE IS NO WAY OUT.
THERE IS NO END.
ESPECIALLY NOT **TODAY.**
A SMASHED WING BEATS IN SLOW MOTION.
THE WAVE OF A HAND CONJURES THE MUSIC OF **VIVALDI** OUT OF FRESH AIR.

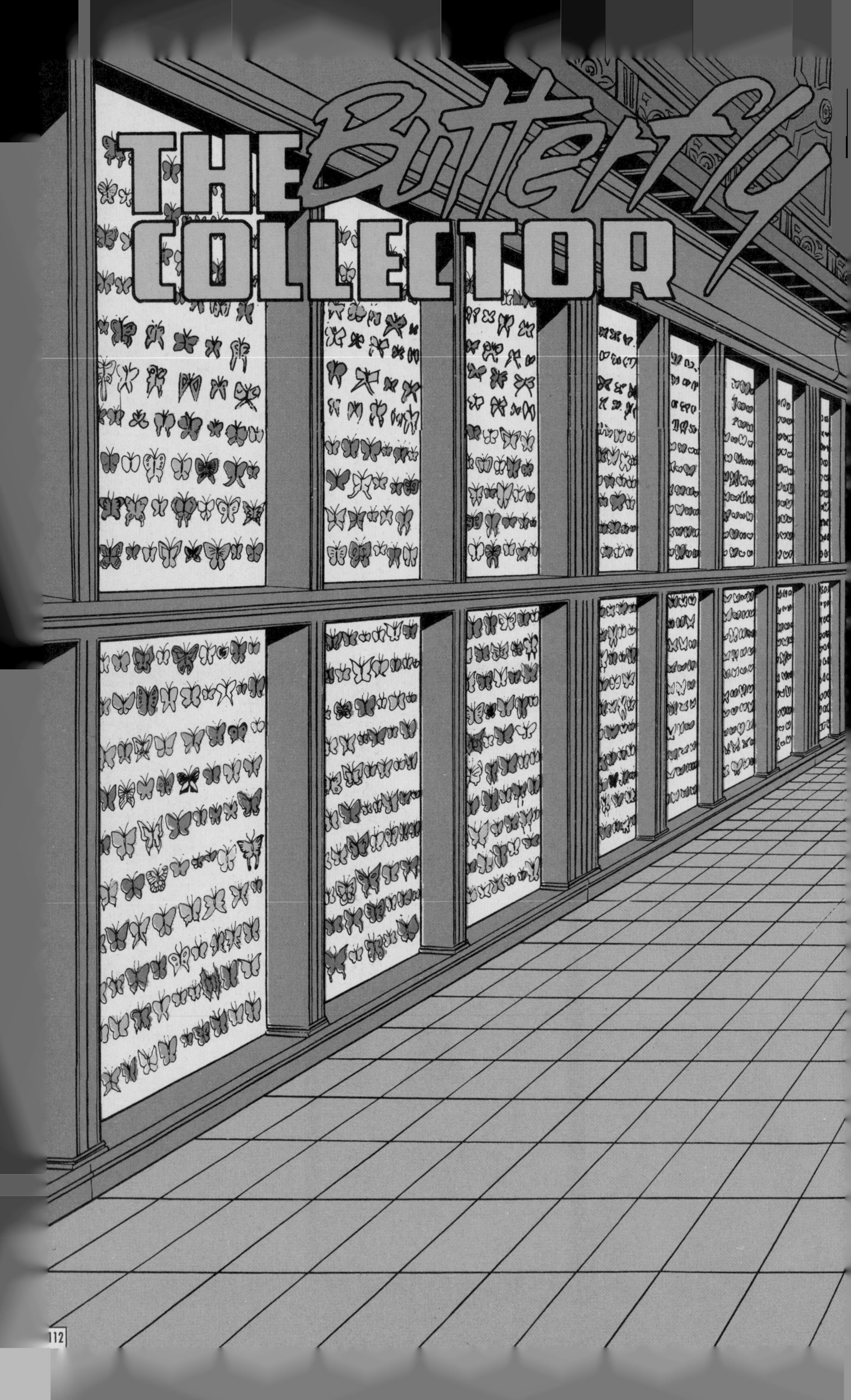
THE Butterfly COLLECTOR

FOR TODAY IS MY WEDDING DAY!

RHODE ISLAND. DOOM PATROL HEADQUARTERS.
THE WIND FROM THE EAST.
GOOD MORNING, JOSHUA.
UNSEASONABLY COLD, DON'T YOU THINK? THE TEMPERATURE DROPPED DRAMATICALLY...
...AT A QUARTER AFTER THREE LAST NIGHT.
YEAH.
WHAT IS THAT?
IT'S WHAT WE CALL THE LORENZ ATTRACTOR--A COMPUTER IMAGE OF THE INFINITE HIDDEN STRUCTURE CONTAINED IN A CHAOTIC STREAM OF DATA.
A PICTURE OF THE RULES THAT GOVERN WEATHER, FOR INSTANCE.
I'LL TAKE YOUR WORD FOR IT.
WEATHER IS COMPLETELY UNPREDICTABLE, YOU SEE. THEORETICALLY, A CATASTROPHIC CYCLONE IN BANGLADESH CAN BE TRACED BACK TO SOMETHING AS SIMPLE AS THE TINY PERTURBATIONS MADE IN THE AIR BY THE WING OF A BUTTERFLY IN SOUTH AMERICA.
IT'S A CHAIN REACTION OF EVENT AND CONSEQUENCE THAT...
YEAH, LISTEN, IT'S NOT THAT I DON'T WANT TO TALK METEOROLOGY WITH YOU OR ANYTHING, BUT I REALLY CAME UP TO TELL YOU THAT I'D... WELL, I'D LIKE TO ACCEPT YOUR OFFER.
I'D LIKE TO STAY WITH THE DOOM PATROL.
114

FINE.
THAT'S UNDER THE TERMS WE AGREED; I'M WITH THE TEAM PURELY IN A *MEDICAL* CAPACITY.
NO MORE SUPER-HERO STUFF.
OKAY?

FINE. I SAID "FINE," JOSHUA.
YOUR EXPERTISE WILL BE MOST WELCOME.

I THINK IT'S ESSENTIAL THAT THE DOOM PATROL HAS SOME GOOD, SOLID IN-HOUSE BACK-UP.
AND NOW I'D LIKE YOU TO MEET THE *SECOND* MEMBER OF WHAT I'VE COME TO THINK OF AS THE "OUTER TEAM."

SHE ARRIVED TEN MINUTES AGO.
I BELIEVE YOU ALREADY KNOW ***DOROTHY SPINNER.***

...HI...

...REALLY, ELEANOR... I CAN'T HANDLE THIS... I...
IT'S...YOU COME HERE COVERED IN BANDAGES AND YOU'RE HALF-MAN, HALF-WOMAN AND YOU EXPECT ME JUST TO... JUST TO...
IT'S SICK.
THIS THING IS SO SICK.
I REMEMBER THE DOLLS. I... DIDN'T WE... DIDN'T I COLLECT DOLLS?
DOLLS?
DOLLS?
LOOK!
LOOK AT THIS!

...BLOOD...
SYMBOLIC, RIGHT... JUST LIKE A MOVIE... IT'S...

REMEMBER THAT OLD GERMAN GUY TOOK THIS THE DAY BEFORE YOU HURT YOUR FOOT GOING UP TO THE ACROPOLIS ?
YOU ERE STUCK N THE HOTE FOR THREE AYS... PLAYING TRIVIAL PURSUIT ...I...

THIS IS US!

THIS IS US!

THE DOLLS ARE VERY BEAUTIFUL, DAN.
I'D LIKE TO TAKE ONE AWAY WITH ME.

THAT'S IF YOU DON'T MIND.

...AND YOU REMEMBERED TO BRING THOSE TAPES, YEAH?
HOW MANY TIMES DO I HAVE TO TELL YOU, CLIFF? I BROUGHT EVERYTHING!
RISON GENERAL HOSPITA
I DON'T KNOW... I CAN'T SEE COUNTRY MUSIC BRINGING ANYONE OUT OF A COMA. I MEAN, IT'D PUT ME INTO ONE...
I WISH I'D NEVER WORN THIS COSTUME...
FLAUNT IT, BABY, FLAUNT IT!
FOURTH FLOOR, PAL. I'M HERE TO COMPLAIN TO MY PLASTIC SURGEON.
UP.
THAT'S IT THERE...
CLIFF! SOMETHING'S WRONG.
HEY, WHAT'S GOING ON HERE? WE'RE CLIFF STEELE AND CRAZY JANE FROM THE DOOM PATROL. WE'RE HERE TO SEE RHEA JONES.
THIS IS HER ROOM, ISN'T IT?
YES...WELL ...I THINK YOU'D BETTER...
WE'VE HAD SOME PROBLEMS.

...SO WHAT DO YOU THINK OF THE NEW DOOM PATROL HEADQUARTERS, DOROTHY?
PRETTY SMART, HUH?
I DIDN'T SEE THE OLD ONE, MR. CLAY.

NO...NO, I GUESS YOU DIDN'T ...SO, WHAT BRINGS YOU OUT HERE, ANYWAY?
WELL, IT WAS PROFESSOR CAULDER, I GUESS. HE CALLED MY DAD AFTER THE INVASION AND ALL.

HE MUST HAVE HEARD ABOUT WHAT HAPPENED TO ME WHEN THE GENE BOMB WENT OFF.

YEAH? SO WHAT DID HAPPEN?
OH... WELL, IT WAS KIND OF...

WAIT A MINUTE!
I'M SORRY, DOROTHY, BUT IS IT JUST MY EARS OR DO YOU HEAR SOMETHING? KIND OF LIKE SQUISHY...

...FOOT-STEPS...
OH MY GOD.

GET BACK, DOROTHY!
GET BACK!
FOR GOD'S SAKE, DOROTHY! I JUST SAID...
YOU GO AWAY!
LEAVE US ALONE!
YOU HEAR ME NOW?
GO AWAY!
I'M REAL SORRY, MR. CLAY.
SOMETIMES THESE THINGS JUST JUMP RIGHT OUT OF MY HEAD.

...WE WERE GOING TO GET MARRIED. TWO MONTHS TIME.
YOU'RE TAKING ME APART, ELEANOR...

REBIS. NOT ELEANOR.
LISTEN, JUST GO, WILL YOU?
PLEASE JUST...

OH, GOD, ELEANOR.
I DON'T...
WHAT AM I GOING TO DO?

WHAT AM I GOING TO DO?

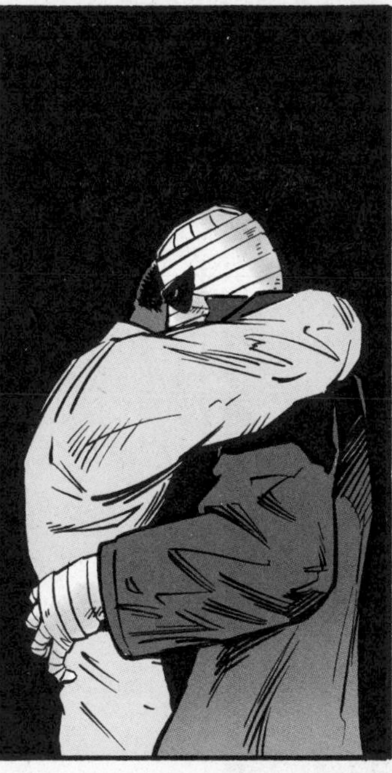

DON'T GET BLOOD ON THE COAT.

WE THINK IT ALL HAPPENED SOMETIME BETWEEN THREE AND FOUR THIS MORNING.

RHEA WAS IN A **COMA!** HOW COULD SHE HAVE DONE THIS? I MEAN...

JONES, RHEA

THERE'S SOMETHING HERE!

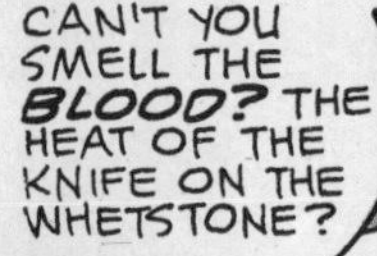

IT TOOK RHEA.
A HOUSE WITH NO DOORS... I CAN'T...
BOOK-STORE!
QUICK! WHERE'S THE NEAREST BOOKSTORE?
IT'S... AH ...IT'S JUST...
OH.
OH, WHAT ARE YOU DOING TO ME?
READING YOUR MIND. YOU SPEAK TOO SLOWLY.
BOOKSBOOKS INEEDBOOKS
I'D... AH... I'D BETTER STAY WITH HER.
JANE!
JANE, COME BACK!
WHAT D'YOU THINK YOU'RE...
BEEP
HONK!
EATON'S BOOKSTALL
ADVENTURES OF BARON MUNCHAUSEN ON SALE
MAY
20% OFF EATON'S

Dada
BOOKS BOOKS BOOKS
NATURE'S END
DHALGREN
OW.
DUMB MOVE.
LISTEN, IT'S OKAY.
SHE'S A SUPER-HERO.
SALE
JANE... I... YOUR HAIR'S FULL OF GLASS...
HURTS LIKE HELL.
STILL, GOT WHAT I NEED.
NATURE'S END
20% OFF

...IT'S THE DOOM PATROL, OKAY? HERE'S THE ADDRESS. WE'LL TAKE CARE OF THE DAMAGE.
SORRY ABOUT THE WRITING. ROBOT FINGERS, YOU KNOW?

AND REMEMBER, KIDS: DON'T WALK THROUGH PLATE GLASS WINDOWS!

SKREE
HONK!
HONK!
JANE!
JANE! WAIT!

11 12 14 15 16
JANE!

Ding
DAMN!

Phon
Phone
Phone

SCISSORS.
I NEED A PAIR OF SCISSORS.

...CHIEF?...YEAH, LISTEN...SOMETHING WEIRD'S HAPPENED DOWN AT THE HOSPITAL...
YEAH... RHEA'S VANISHED ...POSSIBLY ABDUCTED.

RANDOM WORDS. CUT PHRASES.
IT'S A KIND OF DIVINATION, LIKE CASTING THE RUNES OR READING THE FLIGHT OF BIRDS.
ONLY WITH WORDS.
SNIP
SNIP

...AS SOON AS REBIS GETS BACK, SEND HIM DOWN HERE... YEAH...
I'VE GOT A FEELING ABOUT THIS ONE, CHIEF...
...YEAH... STRAIGHT AWAY...

SHUFFLE THEM.
SEE HOW THEY FALL? LIKE SNOW.

EXCUSE ME, ARE YOU WITH THAT WOMAN WHO...
DON'T WORRY ABOUT IT. SHE'S A SUPER-HERO.

...YOU SEE NOW? THE PRESENCE BEGINS TO REVEAL ITSELF IN THE CASUAL REARRANGEMENT OF THE TEXT FRAGMENTS.
IT BECOMES A KIND OF SEANCE. TO CONTACT THE LIVING.
LISTEN:
STRANGE DOCTORS OF PAIN.
HISTORY, WAKE UP!
ALCHEMY STARTS IN THE HOUR OF THE KNIFE. THE BUTTERFLY LABYRINTH WAS NO ACCIDENT.
THE SKINNED RETINA I PLUCKED FROM MY MOTHER'S FOREHEAD WHEN A BOY.
O HAVE YOU SEEN THE DEVLE WITH HIS VIOLET MIKERSCOPE AND AESTHETIC SCALPUL.
THE SATANIC DR. STANLEY FAVOURS THE ENTRAILS OF FEAR.
THE APPEAL OF THE MICHAELMAS GIRLS SUBJECTED TO THE MURDERING MARTYRS.
ONLY A GRAVE IN MITRE SQUARE.
THE MORTUARY IN OLD MONTAGUE STREET IN WHICH HE WEIGHS THE SOULS OF FIREWORKS OR GALAXIES.
THE AUTUMN OF TERROR FALLS TO PIECES. RUTHLESS PROPHECIES OF THE SECRET CITY. THE BLUE SIGNATURE OF STRANGE ATTRACTORS.
GOOD-NIGHT, MARY.
UP SIDLES JACK.
THE WORD IS MURDER, OLD BOSS.

YOU SEE?
...JACK THE RIPPER?...
THE WORDS ARE THE KEY... THE NAMES OF THE VICTIMS OPEN THE DOOR... MARY ANNE NICHOLS.
ANNIE CHAPMAN. ELIZABETH STRIDE. CATHERINE EDDOWES. MARIE JEANETTE KELLY.
RHEA JONES.
R.J. R.J.
RED JACK.
MY GOD

JANE, WAIT! DON'T JUST GO...
LISTEN... WE'LL...WE'LL TRY NOT TO BE TOO LONG.
OKAY?
NO, DON'T... WAIT...
I HAVE TO SEE... WE CAN'T JUST...
...OH...
PRIVATE
412A

IT CAN'T BE THE *SCISSORMEN* AGAIN, CAN IT?
JANE?
REBIS?
JANE?
HELL!

THE MUSIC COMES IN WAVES.
FREAKBEAT VIVALDI SAMPLED AND SPLICED TOGETHER WITH THE SCREAMS OF MURDERED WOMEN AND BUTTER-FLIES.
AND WEDDING BELLS.
PETALS?
THE CLAMOR OF WEDDING BELLS.
YOU'RE

THE WEDDING'S OVER.
RHEA?

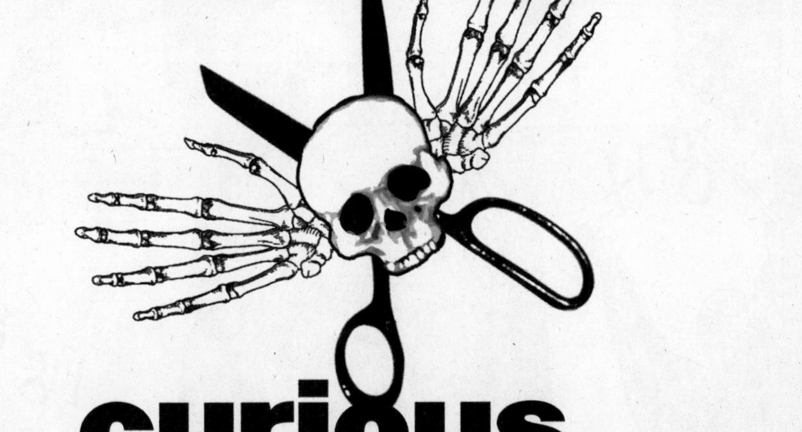

"You're a **curious** creature, aren't you? A thing of parts."

THE DOOM PATROL
DC
NEW FORMAT
24
JUL 89
US $1.50
CAN $1.85
UK 80p
Fig. 14
Fig. 15
a.
CASE • Hanna
THE HOUSE THAT JACK BUILT
GRANT MORRIS
RICHARD CA
SCOTT HAN

LIGHT.
WE NEED LIGHT.
THERE MUST BE A SWITCH.
ARE YOU SURE?
TRY HERE.
WHERE?
HERE. ON THE WALL.
IT'S HERE SOME...
AH.
THERE.

THE HOUSE THAT JACK BUILT

ULTRAVIOLET STROBE CHANDELIERS.
NICE.
WHAT'S THAT MUSIC?
SOUNDS LIKE **VIVALDI.** SCRATCH MIX. DIGITAL SAMPLING.
OH, RIGHT.
SO. WHAT NOW?
SEARCH FOR THE OTHERS?
THEY MUST BE IN HERE.
MMUUUUU
SOME...
...WHERE...

...CLIFF?
REBIS?
WHAT THE BUTLER SAW 6P

MA-MA
MA-MA
MA-MA
EEUURR!
WHAT THE BUTLER SAW

...WHAT IS THIS PLACE?
THIS? THIS IS MY HOUSE. AND I BELIEVE YOU KNOW MY WIFE. NOT IN THE BIBLICAL SENSE, OF COURSE.
"JUST RHEA AND ME AND BABY MAKES THREE..."
"...WE'RE HAPPY IN MY BLUE HEAVEN..."
WHAT?
THIS IS INSANE! YOU CAN'T MARRY HER. SHE...SHE'S IN A COMA, FOR GOD'S SAKE!
ADMITTEDLY, HER CONVERSATION IS A LITTLE DULL.
BUT THEN AGAIN, LOVE CONQUERS ALL.
I'VE HAD ENOUGH OF THIS CRAP!

KKRK
TEMPER!
I SHOULD REALLY INTRODUCE MYSELF. RED JACK'S THE NAME. YOU MAY, HOWEVER, BE MORE FAMILIAR WITH MY OTHER TITLE...
WUHH
KKKRAKK
GOD.
PLEASED TO MEET YOU.
UFF!
KKKK

oh
POOR BUTTERFLIES.

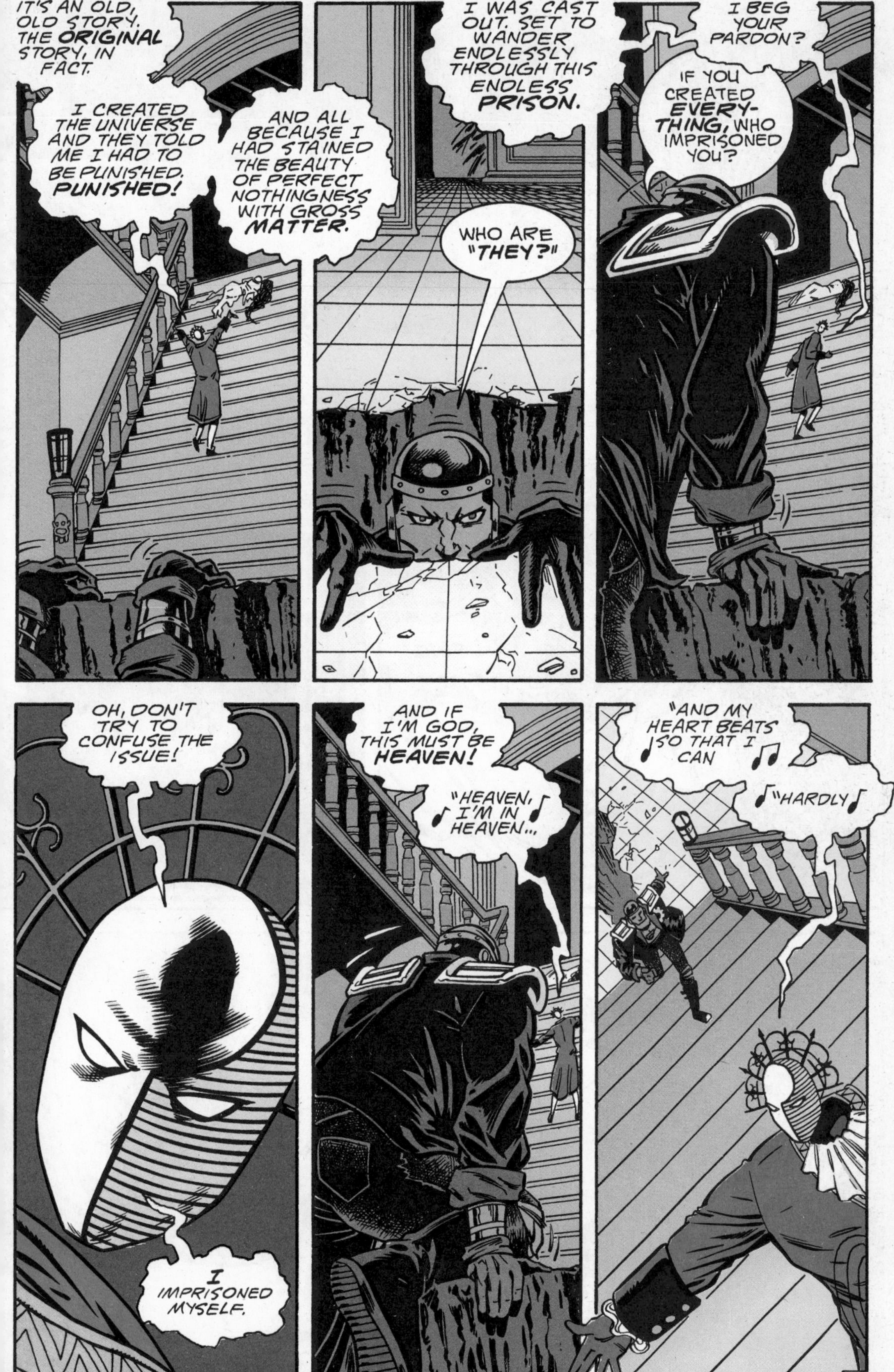
IT'S AN OLD, OLD STORY. THE ORIGINAL STORY, IN FACT.
I CREATED THE UNIVERSE AND THEY TOLD ME I HAD TO BE PUNISHED. PUNISHED!
AND ALL BECAUSE I HAD STAINED THE BEAUTY OF PERFECT NOTHINGNESS WITH GROSS MATTER.
I WAS CAST OUT. SET TO WANDER ENDLESSLY THROUGH THIS ENDLESS PRISON.
WHO ARE "THEY?"
I BEG YOUR PARDON?
IF YOU CREATED EVERY-THING, WHO IMPRISONED YOU?
OH, DON'T TRY TO CONFUSE THE ISSUE!
I IMPRISONED MYSELF.
AND IF I'M GOD, THIS MUST BE HEAVEN!
♪ "HEAVEN, I'M IN HEAVEN... ♪
"AND MY HEART BEATS ♪ SO THAT I CAN ♫
♪ "HARDLY ♪

"... SPEAK..."
KAWHAK
KKRUNCH
SING MY FAVORITE SONG, RHEA. YOU KNOW THE WORDS.
"ALONG CAME JACK, NOT MY TYPE AT ALL... YOU'D MEET HIM ON THE STREET AND NEVER NOTICE HIM..."
SING!
OHHHH
RHEA?
RHEA?
NO!
"HE'S JUST MY
"JACK!"
CHK

UUMMUUU
RELEASE THE NEGATIVE SPIRIT!
THE NEGATIVE SPIRIT.
WHAT?
THE NEGATIVE SPIRIT!
SNAP
SNAP
SNAP
SNAP
MMMUUUUUU
HFF
WELL?
SHALL WE GO?
IV

DON'T FRET.
NOTHING ACTUALLY DIES HERE. HERE, THERE IS ONLY SUFFERING.
PAIN SUSTAINS MY EXISTENCE.
BUTTERFLIES. DO YOU LIKE BUTTERFLIES?
PRETTY, FRAGILE THINGS WITH WINGS LIKE CHURCH WINDOWS.
THEY HAVE FAIRLY RUDIMENTARY NERVOUS SYSTEMS, OF COURSE. THAT'S WHY I NEED SO MANY.
PINNED IN THEIR MILLIONS, FEEDING ME WITH THEIR AGONY.
I'VE BEEN COLLECTING THEM FOR A LONG TIME.
ONCE IN EVERY HUNDRED YEARS, THE ENDLESS ORBITING PATH OF MY WANDERING TAKES ME INTO THAT PART OF MY HOUSE WHICH IS YOUR WORLD.
ONE HUNDRED YEARS AGO... HAUNTING THE FOGBOUND, GASLIT STREETS OF WHITECHAPEL.
OH, I WAS JACK THEN...
...RED JACK, SPRING-HEELED JACK, SAUCY JACK, JACK FROM HELL, TRADE-NAME...

JACK THE RIPPER.
URRRZZ
I HAD A PLAN, YOU UNDERSTAND.
THE OLD URGE TO CREATE WAS STILL STRONG.
SO I CUT THEM UP.
ANNIE AND CATHERINE AND PRETTY MARY
LONG LIZ AND SWEET MARIE JEANETTE IN THE FEVER ROOM. WITH MY KNIFE.
DIVIDING THEIR FLESH.
THEY WERE NOTHING.
CHEAP HARLOTS AND SLEEPWALKERS.
DID I SAY SLEEPWALKERS?
STREETWALKERS. SLEEPWALKERS. THEY'RE ALL THE SAME TO ME.
I THOUGHT THAT IF I CUT THEM UP AND REASSEMBLED THE FLESH IN NEW CONFIGURATIONS...
WELL, I THOUGHT THAT I COULD CREATE A BEAUTIFUL NEW FORM OF LIFE. SOMETHING BETTER THAN HUMAN.
PLAN DIDN'T WORK.
TYPICAL.

OH, NOT ANOTHER ONE!
YOU'RE ALL WASTING YOUR TIME.
CCRRRAKKK
RRREBISSZZ!
LOOK-K-K OUT FOR
OH.
UHNNNNN
URRR
SEE?

ANYWAY.
WHAT WAS I SAYING ?
YES. YES... I'VE DECIDED TO MARRY. ALL WORK AND NO PLAY MAKES JACK A DULL BOY, AFTER ALL.

I CAN'T SAY I CHOSE RHEA FOR HER PERSONALITY, BUT I SAW HER POTENTIAL. I RECOGNIZED WHAT SHE WAS BECOMING WHILE SHE SLEPT.

AND LOOK AT THOSE HIPS!
THINK OF THE CHILDREN WE'LL HAVE.

HOW MANY TIMES MUST I TELL YOU?
HANDS

OFF!

AWWW SZZZH...

KAPOW

RRRAAAGH!
THAT'S ALL VERY EASY FOR YOU TO SAY.
ARRR RGGH, HHHH!
AHHHH
WAIT! WHAT ARE YOU DOING?
YOU CAN'T JUST SHUT DOWN YOUR NERVOUS SYSTEM LIKE THAT! I NEED YOUR PAIN!
YOU'RE A CURIOUS CREATURE, AREN'T YOU? A THING OF PARTS.
STRANGE... I FEEL THERE'S SOMETHING NOT QUITE RIGHT ABOUT YOU. AN ABSENCE.
...SOMETHING MISSING...

ARRRR
AHHH.
STEADY. STEADY.
DO YOU NEVER LEARN?
CAN'T YOU JUST STOP?
SKAKT
UHH?

CRASH
DON'T WORRY.
YOU'LL LOOK BACK AND LAUGH.
AS FOR YOU!
THERE.
NOT SO CLEVER NOW, EH?
NOT SO CLEVER NOW!
MY KNIFE.
WHERE'S MY

AAAAAAAAAA
OH.
OH, RHEA... WE COULD HAVE DISCUSSED THIS...
AHHH... IS THIS IT?
IS... THIS... WHAT IT FEELS LIKE?
...THIS EMPTYING... BLACK FIREWORKS INSIDE... AND WIND...
..., SUCH... A WIND...
...ROARING... A HURRICANE...
...OF WINGS?...

...NO...NO, DON'T LEAVE ME...YOU'LL DIE...WITH ME YOU LIVE FOREVER...
...THIS ISN'T HAPPENING...
...IT CAN'T...
...NO PAIN...NO PAIN ANYWHERE ...LIGHT FAILS... MUSIC FALTERS...
...I NEED PAIN...
OH, THE DARK COMES ON IN WAVES...
I...I...THOUGHT I WAS PART OF THE GRAND STORY...
THE STORY THAT... THAT WOULD AT LAST GIVE MEANING TO THIS SENSELESS TRAJECTORY... THE LOOP AND SPIN OF BEING...
INSTEAD...INSTEAD I HAVE LEARNED A HORRIBLE TRUTH OF... EXISTENCE...
SOME STORIES HAVE
NO
MEANING.
oh, bugger...
CLIFF?

CLIFF? HAVE I MISSED SOME-THING?
N-N-NOTHING MUCHZZZ.
DID YOU ZZSET THE -CRRK- BUTTER-FLIES FREE?
UH-HUH.
WAS THAT OKAY?
YEAH. YEAH.
SZZMART MOVE, KI-KI-CRAZY JANE.
HE WAS -CRZZZ- LYING, WASN'T HE?
YOU D-D-DON'T REALLY THINK HE WAS... GOD?
COULDN'T CARE LESS.

...ZZZS' FUNNY, ISN'T IT?
HILARIOUS.
NO, I M-M-MEAN THE WAY ÷CCRK÷ THE WAY RED JI-JACK MUST HAVE B-B-BEEN HERE FOR SZZO LONG AND THEN ÷CRRZ÷ IT'S OVER FOR HIM SZZO KI-KI-QUICKLY.
THE KNIFE ÷CRRKK÷ THE B-B-BUTTER-FLIES.
THE THINGS THAT KI-KI-KILLED HIM WERE ÷CRKK÷ WERE HERE ALL THE T-T-TIME, YOU KNOW?
WE N-N-NEVER SEE THE ÷CRZZ÷ THINGS THAT ARE R-R-RIGHT UNDER OUR N-N-N OUR NOSES, DO WE? STILL...
THAT'SZZ LIFE, I GUESS.
THERE'SZZ ÷CRRK÷ ONLY ONE THING THAT'SZZ RI-RI-REALLY B-BOTHER... BOTHERING ME ÷CRZZZ÷ NOW.
HOW DO WE GET OUT?

DETROIT. HOT SKIES. EMERGENCY SIRENS. FALLING GLASS. ALCOHOLIC SWEAT.

LLOYD JEFFERSON.

din do nuthin no way din do it

"You shot your imaginary friends? With **what?"**

"An imaginary gun! What else?"

NEW FORMAT

25
AUG 89

US $1.50
CAN $1.85
UK 80p

THE DOOM PATROL

BY MORRISON, BRAITHWAITE & NYBERG

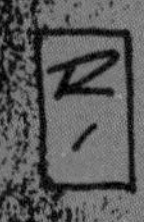

EVERY WISH HAS ITS PRICE.
Imaginary Friends

BEFORE I GO, JOSHUA-- ***MAXWELL LORD*** OF THE ***JUSTICE LEAGUE*** CALLED YESTERDAY.

APPARENTLY A NUMBER OF ITEMS WERE LEFT BEHIND IN THE ***SOUVENIR ROOM*** WHEN THE ORIGINAL LEAGUE ***ABANDONED*** THIS COMPLEX.

LORD IS PARTICULARLY INTERESTED IN SOMETHING CALLED A ***MATERIOPTIKON.***

A ***WHAT?***

MATERIOPTIKON. AS FAR AS I UNDERSTAND, IT'S A DEVICE THAT ***DOCTOR DESTINY*** USED TO EXTERNALIZE THE SUBCONSCIOUS.

THE LEAGUE RECENTLY HAD SOME KIND OF TEDIOUS SKIRMISH WITH DESTINY...

...AND LORD IS ANXIOUS TO RETRIEVE ALL COPIES OF THE MATERIOPTIKON.

YOU WOULDN'T MIND TAKING A LOOK IN THE SOUVENIR ROOM, WOULD YOU?

IF YOU LIKE.
YOU KNOW, YOU DON'T SEEM TOO CONCERNED ABOUT THE FACT THAT CLIFF AND THE OTHERS HAVE BEEN MISSING FOR ALMOST TWO DAYS...
I'M NOT. WHEREVER THEY ARE, THE DOOM PATROL CAN TAKE CARE OF THEMSELVES.
YOU SHOULD KNOW THAT, JOSHUA.
YEAH.
SO WHERE ARE YOU HEADED?
WASH-INGTON. WITH A NEW PRESIDENT IN THE WHITE HOUSE...
...MY MY GOVERNMENT COMMITMENTS ARE AT AN END. ALL THAT REMAINS IS TO CLEAR UP A FEW ITEMS OF BUSINESS.
THERE'S ALSO THE MATTER OF SOME DEBTS THAT ARANI ACCUMULATED DURING HER TERM AS TEAM LEADER.
YOU KNOW, I NEVER COULD FIGURE OUT WHY ARANI SHOULD HAVE CLAIMED TO BE YOUR WIFE IN THE FIRST PLACE...
THE POOR WOMAN WAS HOPELESSLY INSANE, JOSHUA.
WHAT OTHER EXPLANATION DO YOU REQUIRE?
CAN YOU IMAGINE ME MARRIED?
I MEAN, REALLY!
YEAH.

...UM... MR. CLAY...
EXCUSE ME, MR. CLAY...
CONFESSIONS of an ENGLISH OPIUM EATER
CONFESSIONS of an English OPIUM EATER -- De Quincey

DOROTHY! HI! HOW ARE YOU?
YOU SETTLING IN OKAY?

WELL, NOT REALLY. THERE'S SOMETHING WRONG WITH THE TEEVEE.
I DIDN'T REALLY WANT TO BOTHER YOU...

HEY, NO PROBLEM! I'M NOT TOO GREAT WITH TELEVISIONS, BUT I'LL TAKE A LOOK.

IT COULD BE THIS WEIRD WEATHER WE'VE BEEN HAVING.
I DON'T THINK SO, MR. CLAY.
I DON'T THINK IT'S WEATHER.
... AND IT'S THE SAME ON EVERY CHANNEL.
YEAH, THAT DOES SOUND A LITTLE STRANGE.
SEE?
IT'S BEEN LIKE THAT FOR A WHOLE DAY NOW. IT'S REAL BORING.
A WHOLE DAY?
AND YOU DIDN'T TELL US?
I DIDN'T WANT TO BOTHER ANYONE.

YOU MEAN THERE'S BEEN NOTHING ON THE SCREEN BUT THIS ROOM AND THIS TABLE?
ON EVERY CHANNEL? FOR A WHOLE DAY?
YOU MUST HAVE BEEN PRETTY BORED.
IT WAS OKAY FOR A WHILE. I KEPT THINKING SOMETHING MIGHT HAPPEN.
IT'S WEIRD. MAYBE WE'RE PICKING UP SOME STRAY SATELLITE TRANSMISSION.
NAH.
I DON'T KNOW. IT'S TOO BAD THE CHIEF JUST LEFT...
YOU LIKE TV, DON'T YOU? I GUESS YOU'LL FEEL KIND OF LOST WITHOUT IT.
YEAH. I USED TO WATCH IT ALL THE TIME BACK AT THE FARM. I NEVER DID GET OUT MUCH.
Y'KNOW... LOOKING THE WAY I DO AND ALL...
SO WHAT HAPPENED WITH SCHOOL? YOUR MOM AND DAD TEACH YOU?
MA AND PA DIDN'T EVER HAVE TIME FOR THAT.
NO. MY IMAGINARY FRIENDS TAUGHT ME.

WHAT?
SURE.
THEY TAUGHT ME HOW TO READ AND WRITE AND ALL KINDS OF STUFF.
IMAGINARY FRIENDS?
UH-HUH.
DIDN'T YOU HAVE IMAGINARY FRIENDS, MR. CLAY?
DOESN'T **EVERY-ONE?**
I GUESS... *YEAH*, WELL, NOW THAT YOU MENTION IT... BACK IN THE **ORPHANAGE**, I USED TO IMAGINE I HAD A KIND OF MAGICAL DOG.
MR. VINEGAR. I USED TO TALK TO HIM ALL THE TIME.
I HAD A WHOLE **FAMILY;** THERE WAS **DAMN ALL**, THE DADDY, **DARLING-COME-HOME**, WHO WAS LIKE THE MOM, AND THIS LITTLE KID CALLED **FLYING ROBERT.**
THEY USED TO PLAY WITH ME AND TELL ME STORIES.
IT WAS REAL FUN AT FIRST.
THIS IS THE FIRST TIME I'VE HEARD OF SOMEONE BEING ***EDUCATED...***
...BY IMAGINARY PEOPLE.

YEAH, WELL, IT GOT SO I DIDN'T LIKE THE STORIES THEY STARTED TO TELL ME.
THEY WERE GIVING ME BAD DREAMS.
THEY TOLD ME ABOUT THE LITTLE MERMAID AND ABOUT THE GIRL WHO COULDN'T STOP DANCING TILL THEY CUT OFF HER FEET...
SO I SHOT THEM.
YOU SHOT YOUR IMAGINARY FRIENDS?
WITH WHAT?
AN IMAGINARY GUN! WHAT ELSE?

I TOLD THEM I WANTED TO SHOW THEM SOMETHING. THEN I TOOK THEM 'ROUND BEHIND THE BARN AND I SHOT THEM.
WELL, I SUPPOSE THAT'S ONE WAY OF DOING IT...
WHAT AGE WERE YOU WHEN THIS HAPPENED?

ABOUT ELEVEN, I GUESS.
ELEVEN?

DOROTHY, LISTEN... THE CHIEF ASKED ME TO CHECK SOMETHING OUT AND I'D BETTER DO IT NOW BEFORE I FORGET.
CAN WE TALK AGAIN IN A COUPLE OF MINUTES?
SURE.

I'LL BE BACK AS QUICKLY AS I CAN.
DON'T GO AWAY!

SOUVENIR ROOM
SOUVENIR ROOM
FRAGILE
MATERIO
FRAGILE
LIGHT-WEAPON
The KEY'S KEY WEAPON

MATERIOPTIKON
INKY.
INKY.
INKY BOYS.

NO.
OH, NO.
OH, YES.
171

OH, BLACKY, YOU'RE AS BLACK AS INK.
BLACK AS INK.
BLACK AS INK!
BLACK!
BLACK!
WUHH!

"...THE GREAT TALL TAILOR ALWAYS COMES TO LITTLE BOYS WHO SUCK THEIR THUMBS:- AND ERE THEY DREAM WHAT HE'S ABOUT,
"HE TAKES HIS GREAT SHARP SCISSORS OUT!"
AAAAAAA
DOROTHY.

YOU'RE A BAD GIRL, DOROTHY DEAR! WILLFUL AND WICKED WITH A HEAD JUST CRACK-FULL OF DIRTY DIRTY THOUGHTS!
LOOK AT ME WHEN I'M TALKING TO YOU! I'M YOUR DEAR, DEPARTED DARLING-COME HOME, BACK FROM THE DEEP DEEP DEAD TO HAUNT YOU FOR EVER!
ISN'T THAT RIGHT, PA?
I'M DAMN ALL, I AM! MY NEWSPAPER BODY ALIVE WITH FINANCIAL REPORTS AND CROSS-WORD PUZZLES THAT FILL THEMSELVES IN AS IF BY MAGIC!
MY GROTESQUE, SMILING HEAD AND SWARM OF EYES TURNED, AS EVER, IN YOUR DIRECTION! A REMORSELESS AND SURREAL GRIN!
NEEDLE AND THREAD!
FLYING ROBERT!
FLYING ROBERT!
GHOST-BALLOON BABY THING!
UHH!
SEWING UP THE DOOR!
SEWING UP THE DOOR!
IT'S TIME NOW, DOROTHY.
SHOE TIME.

NO! DON'T MAKE ME LOOK AT THEM!
DON'T MAKE ME LOOK!
PUT THEM ON.
PUT ON THE SHOES, DEAR DOROTHY.
PUT ON THE RED SHOES.
BEAUTIFUL RED SHOES.
IT'S JUST LIKE KNIVES, DOROTHY, DEAR. JUST LIKE WALKING ON KNIVES.
REMEMBER THE SHOE SONG?
"I WISH I WERE AN ANGRY SHOE, A BODILESS BALLOON. CUT OFF MY COVENANT WITH GOD THE PAIN OF ORTHOPEDIC GLUE."

DOROTHY.
LET'S GO.
NO!
NO! NO! NO!
DARLING-COME-HOME!

OKAY.
OKAY.
WE'D BETTER **TALK** ABOUT THIS, DOROTHY.

IS IT YOUR PSYCHIC POWER? IS THAT WHAT'S MAKING THESE THINGS HAPPEN? THE WAY YOU MADE THAT **MONSTER** APPEAR WHEN YOU ARRIVED TWO DAYS AGO?
DOROTHY, CAN YOU MAKE THESE THINGS GO AWAY, LIKE YOU DID WITH THE MONSTER?
I **CAN'T!**
I DIDN'T MAKE THIS HAPPEN. I DON'T HAVE POWER THAT ***STRONG.***

I KILLED THEM, MR. CLAY. I KILLED MY IMAGINARY FRIENDS AND THEY'RE REAL MAD ABOUT IT.
IT'S NOT PSYCHIC POWER. THEY'RE REAL AND THEY'VE COME BACK TO PUNISH ME.
FOR GOD'S SAKE, DOROTHY! GHOSTS OF IMAGINARY PEOPLE CAN'T POSSIBLY EXIST!
DON'T SHOUT AT ME!
I FEEL SICK.
I FEEL SICK.
MY GOD! THAT NOISE!
OH, IT'S THEM! IT'S THEM!
THEY'RE COMING TO GET ME! THEY'RE GOING TO MAKE ME WEAR THE SHOES!
THEY'RE GOING TO MAKE ME WEAR THE RED SHOES!
178

OH, MY HEAD! MY HEAD'S SPLITTING OPEN...
URRRRR
EVERYTHING'S GETTING OUT!
THEN LET IT OUT!
TELL ME ABOUT THE RED SHOES, DOROTHY! QUICKLY!
I CAN'T! I CAN'T SAY!
THE BAD WITCH CUT OUT MY TONGUE!
TELL ME!
...I...OH, GOD... I ONLY WANTED RUBY SLIPPERS...RUBY SLIPPERS LIKE DOROTHY IN THE WIZARD OF OZ...
...THAT'S ALL...
I JUST WANTED OTHER KIDS TO LIKE ME AND NOT TO LAUGH AND BE CRUEL AND...AND I WANTED TO BE GROWN UP AND NOT TO BE SCARED ALL THE TIME.
BUT DARLING-COME-HOME SAID I COULDN'T HAVE RUBY SLIPPERS...ONLY RED SHOES...
LIKE IN HANS CHRISTIAN ANDERSEN...
...THE BAD LITTLE GIRL WITH HER FEET CUT OFF AND THE SHOES, THE SHOES STILL DANCING...WITH THE FEET INSIDE... DANCING AT THE CHURCH DOOR IN HORRIBLE RED SHOES...
LIKE THE LITTLE MERMAID WALKING ON KNIVES...AND GINGER ROGERS IN TOP HAT WHEN SHE DANCED SO HARD THAT HER WHITE SATIN SHOES TURNED RED...OH, GOD, I'M RIPPING, I'M RIPPING OPEN...
OHHHH... THE WALLS ARE TURNING TO BUTTER... THEY'RE COMING THROUGH...

EVERYTHING'S TEARING INSIDE... I WAS ELEVEN... BLOOD RUNNING DOWN MY LEGS... TURNING MY WHITE SHOES RED...
I WAS ELEVEN!
NO ONE TOLD ME ABOUT THE BLOOD!
DOROTHY, LISTEN TO ME. PLEASE. WHAT YOU'RE DESCRIBING IS WHAT SOME PEOPLE CALL AN ENGRAM OR AN INVOLUTE, OKAY? IT'S... IT'S A WHOLE BUNCH OF FEELINGS AND EMOTIONS THAT CLUSTER TOGETHER.
THE RED SHOES HAVE TURNED INTO A KIND OF CHARGED-UP SYMBOL...
...OF GROWING UP...
URRRRR
DOROTHY, YOU MUST UNDERSTAND... ONLY YOU CAN MAKE IT STOP!
I DON'T WANT... I DON'T WANT TO GROW UP...I DON'T WANT TO...
I DON'T WANT TO THINK ABOUT... BOYS...
I'M SO UGLY! IT'S NOT FAIR! I DON'T WANT TO GROW UP! IT HURTS!
OH, MR. CLAY, IT HURTS REAL BAD!
YOU HAVE TO FACE IT, DOROTHY! CONFRONT IT!
YOUR MIND IS CAUSING ALL THIS.
IT'S ALL JUST GUILT AND FEAR AND IT'S BEEN EXTERNALIZED IN THE FORM OF THESE IMAGINARY FRIENDS.
IT'S LIKE SOMETHING HAS BOOSTED YOUR OWN IMAGE-MAKING POWER SO THAT...
MY GOD!
WHY DIDN'T I THINK?

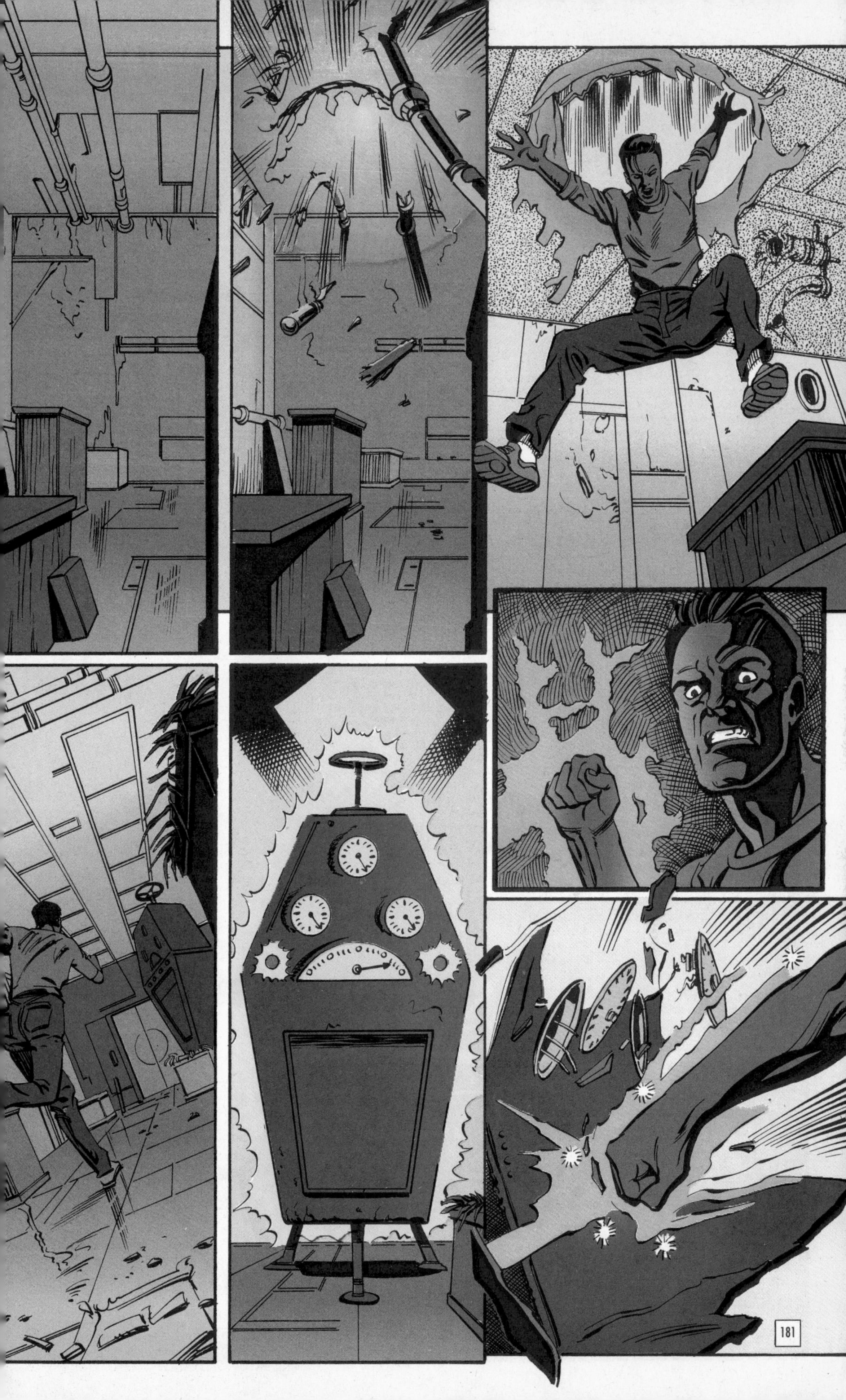

GIVE ME
THE SHOES.

DOROTHY?
YOU PUT THEM ON?
YOU PUT ON THE RED SHOES?
THE *RUBY SLIPPERS,* MR. CLAY.
THEY WERE RUBY SLIPPERS ALL ALONG.
THERE'S NO PLACE LIKE HOME.

EPILOGUE-
SOMEWHERE ELSE.
WELL?
I'M HERE. (LET ME OUT OF THIS PLACE!) SHUT UP!
SORRY. (NO HE'S NOT. HE'S A NO-GOOD LYING SH)
QUIET!
I'M HERE. LIKE YOU SAID. (NO-GOOD)
WHAT DO YOU (CREEP!) WANT?
WHAT DO ANY OF US WANT, MR. SHELLEY? A DECENT STANDARD OF LIVING, A LITTLE RESPECT, A QUARTER TON OF CHOCOLATE MOUSSE.
BUT FOR THE MOMENT WE WANT SIMPLY AND SINCERELY TO... TO WELCOME YOU.
TO THE BROTHER-HOOD OF EVIL.

a word from the author.

(the **following letter** from

grant

morrison

originally appeared in

DOOM PATROL #20

I'll be perfectly honest with you right from the start and admit that I find it incredibly difficult to write this sort of thing. DOOM PATROL editor extraordinaire Bob Greenberger asked me to fill up a couple of pages by introducing myself to the readers of this magazine and waffling on about whatever came to mind. As far as I'm concerned, this pretty much gives me *carte blanche* to bore the pants off everyone by indulging in a series of childhood reminiscences and idle speculations, so, like I always say, "Get out now while you still can!"

Okay. Now that only the real diehards and the serious masochists are left, let's talk about the Doom Patrol.

My involvement with DOOM PATROL came about in the trembling spring of '88 when Bob called me and asked if I'd like to take over the scripting chores on the book, following the departure of Paul Kupperberg. Bob had seen the script for the ARKHAM ASYLUM book that I'm doing with Dave McKean, and he wondered if I could do to the members of the Doom Patrol what I'd done to Batman and the inmates of DC's infamous fictional loony bin.

I was busy with ANIMAL MAN and with my *Zenith* series for *2000 AD* and with all sorts of other things too numerous and too boring to mention, and I wasn't sure if I really wanted to take on another monthly book on top of all this stuff. The more I thought about it, however, the more attractive the idea of revamping the Doom Patrol began to look. What really clinched it was the fact that, when I was a kid, I hardly *ever* read DOOM PATROL; that comic *frightened* me, and the only reason I read any of the stories at all was that there was a certain dark and not-altogether-healthy glamour about those four characters.

That was good enough for me. I decided to write DOOM PATROL.

In these days of angst-ridden mutants and grittily realistic (yawn) urban vigilantes, the Doom Patrol no longer seem quite as extreme as they did back in 1963, but I'm sure that some of you reading this can still recall the genuine frisson that accompanied those early stories. Back in the '60s, when DC super-heroes still sported right-angled jawlines and Boy Scout principles, the Doom Patrol slouched into town like a pack of junkyard dogs with a grudge against mankind. Believe me, this team was *bad* news. An audience more accustomed to the freshly-laundered antics of Wayne Boring's Superman was suddenly confronted by a manic robot with a transplanted human brain, a bandaged pilot who was possessed by a mysterious Negative Being, and an ex-movie starlet whose life and career had been ruined by size-changing powers. To cap it all, this motley crew of complaining misfits was led by an irascible

Adventures in Wonderland, and if you get the chance to see it, jump at it.

The season of Svankmajer films was augmented by "surrealist" classics like Kenneth Anger's *Eaux d'Artifice* and Maya Deren's eerie *Meshes of the Afternoon*, so when the time came to start work on DOOM PATROL, I'd immersed myself in the atmosphere of these weird, irrational worlds and was all set to bring some of that dream-like ambience to the stories I was planning.

Douglas Hofstadter's brilliant book *Gödel, Escher, Bach*, which is an immensely readable voyage into the twilight world of logic and abstract mathematics, was another useful springboard for me (as someone who rarely managed to get beyond writing my name on math exams, I'm doubly grateful to Hofstadter for being so perfectly lucid in his explanations) and some of that material will doubtless find its way into upcoming adventures.

When Rabbit Howls, the astonishing autobiography of multiple personality victim Truddi Chase, was another invaluable source of reference when it came to creating the Crazy Jane character. If you really want to have your mind blown, buy or steal that book and take a peek at what reality looks like from the other side.

Then there were the books on alchemy, the dreams I've used almost directly, the weird little stories told to me by friends and a million other things that I threw into the simmering stew that was the Doom Patrol proposal.

From here on in, we cast ourselves to the tender mercies of you, dear reader.

Anyway...

Basically, my aim is to bring back some of that ol' Doom Patrol magic by stripping the team down to its roots and returning, as quickly as possible, to the freewheeling weirdness that made the early stories so exhilarating. If things go as planned, we'll be hitting you with a rapid turnover of ideas and concepts and unusual villains. In fact, waiting just out of sight in the wings we have the Scissormen, we have Red Jack, we have Mr. Nobody and the New Brotherhood of Evil and, oh, all sorts of other groovy stuff!

I really can't think of anything else to say. I return the space to you, to fill with arned correspondence or Crayola™ squiggles. In taking my leave, I just want to ce you with one final thought:

Remember when all the other kids on the block had Superman and Batman itive role models? Well, if you could only identify with a human brain in a metal a guy wrapped up in bandages, and if you grew up weird, welcome home. mong friends now.

genius in a wheelchair. Add to that a cast of villains that included a disembodied brain and a talking French gorilla and you may begin to understand why those initial Doom Patrol adventures are still looked upon with such fondness by connoisseurs of the strange.

When I sat down to work out what I wanted to do with this book, I decided straight away that I would attempt to restore the sense of the bizarre that made the original Doom Patrol so memorable. I wanted to reconnect with the fundamental, radical concept of the book — that here was a team composed of *handicapped* people. These were no clean-limbed, wish-fulfillment super-adolescents who could model Calvins in their spare time. This was a group of people with serious physical problems and, perhaps, one too many bats in the belfry.

My feeling about the recent incarnation of the Doom Patrol was that, quite simply, they were too normal. I proposed that we create a more or less completely new team, based more clearly on the tight family structure of the original group. Paul Kupperberg, via the INVASION crossover, kindly agreed to kill or maim most of his characters and leave the field clear for me to introduce a Doom Patrol that was a little less comfortable, a little more unsettling, and, I hope, more faithful to the spirit of the Arnold Drake/Bruno Premiani stories of days gone by. Most of all, I wanted to break away from the massive influence that the Claremont/Byrne-era *X-Men* continue to exert over the whole concept of the comic book super-team and to forge a new style that would look forward to the '90s.

Sounds great on paper, doesn't it?

In the end, most of my ideas arrived like Hurricane Gilbert, in one wild w of constant and feverish inspiration. When it was over, I found myself with eno material to take me up to around issue #60, if we can possibly imagine ever that far. At which point — and since I'm rapidly running out of things to s waste some space by mentioning a few of the things that led to the cr new version of the Doom Patrol.

Most certainly a major influence was the work of Jan S films I saw while I was working on my Doom Patrol proposal filmmaker whose films are often mistakenly described as s only surrealist in the strict "super real" sense of that m are generally fairly short; they use a combination of everyday objects; and they present a disturbing v logical constraints. Svankmajer has just released a full

— grant morrison

dear old glasgow toon, scotland

1988

THE GRANT MORRISON LIBRARY

From VERTIGO. Suggested for mature readers.

ANIMAL MAN
A minor super-hero's consciousness is raised higher and higher until he becomes aware of his own fictitious nature in this revolutionary and existential series.

Volume 1: ANIMAL MAN
With Chas Truog, Doug Hazlewood and Tom Grummett

Volume 2: ORIGIN OF THE SPECIES
With Chas Truog, Doug Hazlewood and Tom Grummett

Volume 3: DEUS EX MACHINA
With Chas Truog, Doug Hazlewood and various

THE INVISIBLES
The saga of a terrifying conspiracy and the resistance movement combatting it — a secret underground of ultra-cool guerrilla cells trained in ontological and physical anarchy.

Volume 1: SAY YOU WANT A REVOLUTION
With Steve Yeowell and Jill Thompson

Volume 2: APOCALIPSTICK
With Jill Thompson, Chris Weston and various

Volume 3: ENTROPY IN THE U.K.
With Phil Jimenez, John Stokes and various

Volume 4: BLOODY HELL IN AMERICA
With Phil Jimenez and John Stokes

Volume 5: COUNTING TO NONE
With Phil Jimenez and John Stokes

Volume 6: KISSING MR. QUIMPER
With Chris Weston and various

Volume 7: THE INVISIBLE KINGDOM
With Philip Bond, Sean Phillips and various

DOOM PATROL
The World's Strangest Heroes are reimagined even stranger and more otherworldly in this groundbreaking series exploring the mysteries of identity and madness.

Volume 1:
CRAWLING FROM THE WRECKAGE
With Richard Case, Doug Braithwaite, Scott Hanna, Carlos Garzon and John Nyberg

Volume 2:
THE PAINTING THAT ATE PARIS
With Richard Case and John Nyberg

THE FILTH
With Chris Weston and Gary Erskine

MYSTERY PLAY
With Jon J Muth

SEBASTIAN O
With Steve Yeowell

From VERTIGO
Suggested for mature readers.

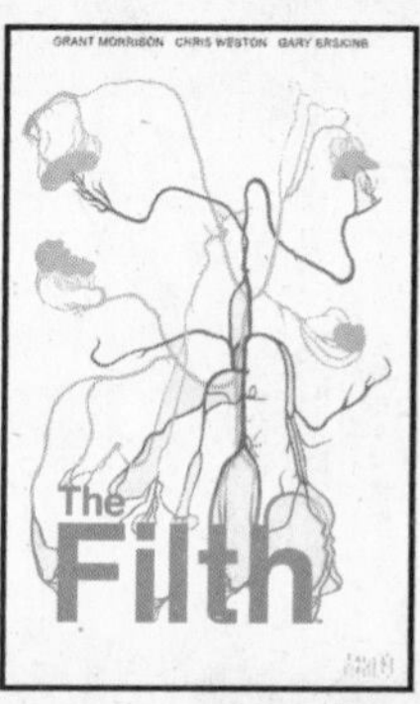

From DC COMICS

BATMAN: ARKHAM ASYLUM
With Dave McKean

JLA: EARTH 2
With Frank Quitely

JLA: NEW WORLD ORDER
With Howard Porter and John Dell

JLA: AMERICAN DREAMS
With Howard Porter, John Dell and various

JLA: ROCK OF AGES
With Howard Porter, John Dell and various

JLA: ONE MILLION
With Val Semeiks, Prentis Rollins and various